POSITIVE PARENTING FOR TODDLERS

EFFECTIVE DISCIPLINE STRATEGIES TO CALM THE CHAOS, CREATE DEEPER CONNECTIONS AND RAISE CONFIDENT, RESPONSIBLE, AND RESPECTFUL HUMANS WITHOUT LOSING YOUR COOL

ALMA ALDRICH

Alma Aldrich

© **Copyright 2022 - All rights reserved.**

The content contained within this book may not be reproduced, duplicated or transmitted without direct written permission from the author or the publisher.

Under no circumstances will any blame or legal responsibility be held against the publisher, or author, for any damages, reparation, or monetary loss due to the information contained within this book, either directly or indirectly.

Legal Notice:

This book is copyright protected. It is only for personal use. You cannot amend, distribute, sell, use, quote or paraphrase any part, or the content within this book, without the consent of the author or publisher.

Disclaimer Notice:

Please note the information contained within this document is for educational and entertainment purposes only. All effort has been executed to present accurate, up to date, reliable, complete information. No warranties of any kind are declared or implied. Readers acknowledge that the author is not engaged in the rendering of legal, financial, medical or professional advice. The content within this book has been derived from various sources. Please consult a licensed professional before attempting any techniques outlined in this book.

By reading this document, the reader agrees that under no circumstances is the author responsible for any losses, direct or indirect, that are incurred as a result of the use of the information contained within this document, including, but not limited to, errors, omissions, or inaccuracies.

Contents

Introduction	1
1. Learning and Unlearning Parenting	10
2. Putting Yourself in Their Little Shoes	34
3. Teaching, Not Taming!	56
4. Praise Is Better Than Prize!	83
5. Paving The Way to Self-Esteem	111
6. Parenting's a Journey—Enjoy the Ride!	129
Conclusion	145
About The Author	150
References	151

Introduction

What you do to children matters. And they might never forget. –Toni Morrison

"What happened to you?" asked my husband in shock after I struggled to open the front door, left four heavy paper bags full of party supplies on the hall floor, and handed him our little girl who was exhausted from sobbing, her chubby face all red and wet. I threw myself on the couch weeping loudly.

Nothing had happened. Nothing different than any other normal afternoon doing groceries with my toddler. But that last time broke me.

It was a Friday afternoon, and the following day we were celebrating our only daughter's second birthday. Just a bunch of friends and family coming over. Still, I wanted everything to look perfect, so I decided to get some decorations, balloons, Doc McStuffins paper napkins, and some party hats. My husband was in the middle of a video call, so I grabbed Lanie and sat her in the car to take her with me. It was almost time for her nap, but she could doze off in the car seat.

When we arrived at the store, and I was almost finished paying for everything that I had bought for her, she spotted a gorgeous silver balloon shaped like an elephant. "Mommy, I want it!" she said in a squeaky voice. "Not now, sweetheart, we already got a lot of stuff." And then she did what she always did: She came up with the classic, parenting textbook temper tantrum. One of the many, only that it was one too much for me. She lay on the floor, crying, and banging my legs with her little fists, and I lost it. I apologized to the cashier, grabbed my daughter, and almost dragged her to the car. The shopping bags were forgotten in the store, I scolded her and I even attempted to pull her hair, although I managed to resist such a horrible impulse. I sat her in her car seat while I kept yelling and she kept screaming. I recall another woman passing by, and knocking on the car window to check on us. That made me even more upset: Who was that stranger and what on Earth gave her permission to judge me?

As I took a long breath of air (possibly, getting ready for some more scolding), I remembered the paper bags left on the store's counter. I remembered the birthday party we had been planning for the past month. And I realized it was all for Lanie! It was supposed to be a happy occasion, a time to create memories, celebrate her life, and bring us closer as a family. *Why was my little girl crying so hard? Why was I yelling at her as I always did? Was this what being a mom really meant?*

I can't remember how I managed to calm down, and with my girl still sobbing, I went back to the store, apologized once more to the cashier, collected the bags with the party supplies, and put them in the trunk of the car. Lanie stopped crying as the moving car put her to sleep. But then *my* eyes were flooded. As I looked into the mirror and I saw her red cheeks with traces of tears, I remembered once more this was supposed to be a happy time, both for her and me. *I don't like being this mom!* That was all I could think of.

And that's what I eventually told my husband when he asked once more what had happened. I hated myself for scolding a two-year-old. I just didn't know what else to do. He stared at me in understanding, and I knew he felt the same way. Although we both had different approaches to parenting, none of us knew the answer. I allowed myself to cry in his supportive arms, then I washed my face and went to

Lanie, who by now had forgotten all about the silver balloon and was trying on a party hat. "I'm sorry, baby," I said. "Now, let's get ready for your birthday party, shall we?"

A lot has changed ever since. I owe it in part to that breaking point in my motherhood, and also to one of my friends, another mum from our daycare group, who came to the party the following day and stayed later to help us clean up. When I told her my story feeling deeply ashamed, she said she had been there. She showed no contempt nor judgment, she just listened. I was grateful for her attitude and I asked her how she managed to keep it all together, she, who had not one, but four kids! And then, she said the two words that changed my family's life for good: *positive parenting*. She recommended a couple of helpful books on the topic, and it became my passion ever since.

I can't underline enough how positive parenting has changed my life for good. Before learning about positive parenting, I thought that the only way of dealing with a toddler and their fussiness was either by punishing them or by surrendering to their wishes. Between being "the mean mum" or "the soft mum," I didn't find the time to enjoy being a mum at all!

If you can relate, you too should learn what positive parenting means, and how you can easily start implementing this philosophy in raising your children.

The Principles of Positive Discipline

For the past decades, experts in psychology have been discussing the best way to raise children, and how to overcome certain difficult stages, such as their infancy or their adolescence. Dr. Jane Nelsen, psychologist and mother of seven, developed the concept of positive discipline through a series of books, which she wrote—along with Lynn Lott and some other co-authors—based on the previous works of Alfred Adler and Rudolf Dreikurs. The first one was an Austrian psychologist in the early 20th century, who worked closely with Sigmund Freud before stepping out to create the school of Individual Psychology.

Together with Dreikurs, another Austrian psychiatrist, Dr. Adler stated a principle that was way ahead of his time: Simply, that children deserved to be treated with respect and dignity, the same as any other person. By the time these two doctors lived and worked, this fact was not widely accepted.

And even today, when we can relate to the sentiment, we don't always put it into practice. How would you feel if your boss took away your cell phone because you didn't complete a task in time? Would you find it appropriate for your husband to force you to finish up a meal despite you not being hungry, only because he spent the last 45 minutes in the kitchen? Would it be okay if someone you don't know scorned you on the bus because you got carried away talking to a friend and you elevated the pitch of your voice for a second?

If we don't find these behaviors acceptable when we are adults, we shouldn't be doing such things to our children either.

However, Adler and Dreikins also emphasized the dangers of spoiling children. We live in a society and we have to respect some ground rules. Can we be firm, yet kind at the same time? We can! That's the main point of the Positive Discipline program developed by Nelsen (Nelsen, 2006). Her main goal was to provide parents all over the world with a set of tools they could implement to raise their children in a firm, yet respectful way.

The three main principles to keep in mind when it comes to positive discipline are:

- That any child that has their basic needs fulfilled also needs to feel significant and important, and to find a connection.

- That every child is inherently good.

- That any misbehaving is a call for attention, and/or help.

As we will see, everything that follows detaches from those three main statements.

Some Benefits of Positive Discipline

Positive discipline does not mean letting your child take control. We have all seen what spoiled children turn into as adults: Most likely, they bump themselves into a wall, as other adults set the boundaries their parents were unable or unwilling to provide. But positive discipline understands that limits should teach children, not punish them.

Among the many benefits my family gained when we embraced positive discipline I can mention the following:

- Our daughter learned to recognize, and better regulate, her own emotions. Eventually, this led to fewer temper tantrums.

- We no longer reacted out of anger, but out of understanding her feelings. Scolding changed to explanations. Fear was no longer a tool. Now, our children listen to us because we have their respect, not because they fear us.

- They show kindness to one another as well as to their peers.

- My oldest daughter has already begun school and she's doing great. Her teacher says she displays much-valued self-confidence and has become a positive leader among her classmates.

- Last but not least, although it may seem unbelievable, my husband and I enjoy being parents! Even sometime later, when we had to deal with not one, but two toddlers at once.

A Little Bit About Myself and why I Wrote This Book

Turning to positive parenting isn't something me and my husband Greg achieved in a day. In fact, we are learning new strategies all the time, and sometimes I still find myself going back to some old scolding, but now I'm not too harsh on myself. I accept I have walked a long road, but every new day as a mom is a new step I have to take. Thus said, I'm so glad we embraced the journey of positive parenting, especially after our family got bigger with our twin boys, Louis and Jack. Positive parenting has helped us adapt to the transition smoothly, understand Lanie's mixed feelings about becoming a big sister, and now it shapes how we deal with our preschoolers.

I decided to write this book because I know how hard parenting can get. We all have ups and downs. Even if we decide to engage in positive parenting, not every day is going to be perfect. I still face daily challenges, especially with my highly energetic twin boys, but now at least I can tell I'm learning from my mistakes and keep trying to improve. I don't have all the answers, and your child is unique. Some of the tactics that have worked for my family may not be suitable for yours. But I am sure you too can benefit from implementing positive parenting.

I shared that story of my break before the birthday party not because I'm proud of it, but to let you know that I've been there. If you are experiencing some similar parenting struggles and you are going through a hard time, know that you are not alone! In the following chapter, we'll analyze why being a parent is so hard for so many people, and what we can do to start making a long-lasting change, both in our children's lives as well as in our mental well-being.

Chapter 1

Learning and Unlearning Parenting

It is easier to build strong children than to repair broken men. –Frederick Douglass

Does positive parenting really have such a huge impact on child development and their parents' well-being? How is it possible that one single parenting style can work for every single family and yet, so many of us aren't implementing it already? What's the catch, then? In this chapter, we will explain other common parenting styles, the influence they have had on most of us towards our family history, and false beliefs about positive parenting that have to be debunked.

We'll also give you some tips on how to start unlearning the old ways and begin implementing the principles of positive parenting.

What You Learned as a Child

Children don't come with a user's guide. It would be great if people could learn how to parent before actually having to take care of a living infant. Most of what we learn about parenting we did from the people around us: That's right, our own parents. If you are reading this book and have a toddler, chances are that your parents are Baby Boomers, or at most Gen-X. And they probably didn't raise you according to the positive parenting philosophy.

The way your folks raised you influences your current relationship with them—if you still have them—but also your way of raising your children. If you have happy childhood memories, you may want to do as your parents did. However, the world in which you grew up is not our world. And that might cause your parenting beliefs and the results you get to collide!

For example, maybe your parents encouraged you to be independent, and so you used to spend most afternoons outside playing with other children in your block. But now you live in an apartment building in a big city, and you can't let your child play unsupervised. You need a couple of hours to do laundry and make dinner, as your mom did 30 years ago. How do you encourage your children's independence without letting them go out by themselves? Easy: You show them an educational program on television, or you hand them a tablet with didactic content. Screen time and outdoor playing with other children lead to very different results, and you are aware of that. But what else could you do?

Other times, when you become a parent you rediscover how much you suffered during your childhood, and you want to become something entirely different. Maybe you grew up with a distant mother, and you turn to attachment parenting ever since your baby is born. Maybe your father was too strict, and therefore you wish to grant your kids everything your parents took away from you. Or maybe you grew up with permissive parents who had trouble setting boundaries, and that caused you difficulties later in life when interacting with your peers. So you become a strict parent, yet your toddler won't listen to you, and every single day becomes a struggle!

Before you blame each of your current parenting struggles on your parents and the way they raised you, take some time to consider they too did the best they could with whatever tool they had. Back then, so many psychological studies we now take for granted weren't common knowledge. There weren't nearly as many parenting books or courses, not to mention the Internet. There were more societal pressures to become a parent, even if deep down your vocation was not raising children. People had kids, well, because they were supposed to! Maybe this was one of your parents' cases, and they did as well as possible. Maybe they longed for a family, and still lacked enough information on how to set some ground rules. Maybe your grandparents were detached parents, and your mum or your dad never learned how to display enough affection.

Think about what they've gone through. Thank them (at least, deep inside) for bringing you into the world and raising you as well as they could. And then yes, make an effort to look back at your own childhood and wonder: How much of your parents are there in you? What things you always took for granted can you change?

The Four Parenting Styles

Most psychologists today acknowledge four different parenting styles, which came from the works of Diana Baumrind. She was a pioneer in the research and one of the first academics to include fathers as well as mothers in her studies. Back in the 1970s,

"Her major contribution was the identification of two central dimensions of parents' behavior—structured expectations and responsiveness—and the discovery that these dimensions in combination revealed three main parenting styles" (University of California, 2018). A fourth style was added to later classifications. What exactly are they?

The Authoritarian Parent

"I'm the adult in charge." "You just do what I say." "Because I said so, period." "That's it, you are grounded, missy." "My house, my rules!" This parenting style is oriented to parental needs and expectations. The structured expectations of these parents are high (they want their kids to be the best in school, they want their rooms spotless, they won't tolerate any discipline problems, they use punishment, etc.) On the other hand, their responsiveness is low, that's why these parents usually become distant from their children, display little affection, and have trouble talking about their—or their children's—emotions.

These parents are well-aware that they are not popular with their kids, but they strongly believe being a parent is not the same as being a friend. They set clear rules and they expect their children to meet them every single time. Perhaps you still believe that this is the right way to go: If you don't provide your children with boundaries, who will? Children already have so much freedom and opportunities nowadays, it's your job as a parent to set them straight, isn't it?

The problem is that children of authoritarian parents often display problematic behaviors: When they are toddlers they could improve their manners out of fear of the consequences, but once they reach their teenage years, they are prompt to becoming either rebellious or depressive. Research from the University of New Hampshire shows that these teens "are more likely to engage in delinquent behaviors (such as smoking, skipping school, and underage drinking) than the children of those with other parenting styles" (Christiano, 2019).

Even if you grew up with authoritarian parents, met their high requirements, and graduated with honors, things may still be less than ideal when it comes to family relationships. Some adults who grew up with authoritarian parents resent them later in life and keep a distant relationship (if any) with their folks. No matter if they meant the best for them, the memories of the past make it hard to forgive them and love them once you are no longer obliged to obey them. If this is your case, you are most likely to attempt a different parenting style: After all, you want your child to love you! This leads us to the second type in the classification.

The Permissive Parent

"Ice cream for lunch? Sounds good to me!" "Did you have a nightmare and you want to sleep in our bed? Don't worry, daddy can sleep on the floor!" "So what if you failed a geography test? This doesn't define you as a person!" Does it sound familiar to you? Perhaps you have struggled so hard not to be an authoritarian figure that you have become a permissive mum or dad. This style falls on the opposite side of the spectrum: Permissive parents display low structured expectations together with high responsiveness. In these families, children are in control instead of the parents. Permissive parents want their kids to feel loved and appreciated exactly the way they are, and therefore, set little to no rules. They allow them to make their own decisions, even if deep down they know they are not the best possible choices.

Although they mean well, permissive parents usually turn out troublesome for their kids. Different studies for the past decade have linked this parenting style with an increase of obesity and cavities in children, proneness to being victims of bullies, teenage drinking, and more stress during the college years; likely because they are not used to being pressured (Christiano, 2019).

Some people reject the whole concept of positive parenting because they have wrongly associated it with the permissive parenting style. They relate being kind and caring with your child with setting no limits. But that's *not* what positive parenting is about (more about this further on).

It is true: Permissive parents are usually loving and caring. They want their children to express their feelings and protect them from the world. They want them so hard to feel happy that sometimes, they forget happiness is something they too should experience. And this is because, besides being tormented by the little tyrants their children can turn themselves into after only receiving all praise and no scolding, permissive parents will usually receive criticism for the way their children behave in public (think about the little boy doing a scandal in the middle of a restaurant because his spaghetti aren't long enough, and daddy discreetly asking the waiter for a burger and fries). Teachers also send these parents notes or citations quite often.

Yet they will stand with their belief that they are acting out of love, that "boys will be boys," that "you learn from your mistakes, after all," or that it is "just a phase." They are not lazy, they are not randomly making all the wrong decisions. These parents are actively *choosing* to let their children be in control because they believe it's the best way to raise them, and that sets them apart from the third parenting style.

The Neglectful Parent

Unlike the two previously discussed parenting styles, this approach to parenting is not a conscious choice. Nobody *decides* their children will be better with an emotionally distant, and/or physically absent parent. It's just life. Single parents who spend most of their time away because they have two jobs and can't make ends meet; parents who are taking care of a sick relative, or have to put all of their attention on a chronically ill child or one with special needs, and therefore cannot give enough attention to the other siblings; or parents who struggle with a mental condition, an addiction, or are unable to take care of their kids... All of them have in common both low structured expectations together with low responsiveness.

While many of us can have a low day, and forget to prepare the costume for the school play, most of the time we try to make it up later. Being distracted or going through a time in which you are too worried about something other than your child doesn't automatically turn you into a neglectful parent. It's keeping the same attitude for most of a kid's childhood. We are talking about those parents who can forget about their child's birthday, or tell themselves they are too busy (or there is no money) to celebrate it. Or parents that, although they receive multiple notes from school, never get to read them, much less attend a parent-teacher meeting. We all have seen the boys in soccer practice that nobody picks up, the little girls with lice all over her shoulders, or those children who learn to cook for their little siblings when they are still at elementary school, not because cooking is fun and engaging, but because it's the only way they can eat something warm.

Sometimes, neglectful parents are also physically abusive, trying to make up for all those boundaries they didn't set. Sometimes, they don't physically harm the children, but don't provide medical attention in time. And even if they somehow manage to take care of their physical well-being, in most cases, they have trouble creating an emotional bond with their children.

As a result, their children suffer more than with any other parenting style. A 2019 research found out that these children are more often than not anxious and/or depressed, antisocial, have difficulties in school—both with their grades as well as in interacting with their peers—and have overall difficulty controlling their emotions (Christiano, 2019).

If you identify with this parenting style, you should ask for help right away. You can get better with social assistance, or psychological treatment. I don't intend to blame you, or to make you feel guilty. Chances are you are going through a lot you cannot manage on your own. Perhaps, your own parents neglected you as a child. In any case, it's never too late to attempt a change and to make a difference in your child's life. And it takes a lot of thinking and self-consciousness to achieve the fourth (and the most desirable) parenting style.

The Authoritative Parent

What do you get when you combine the high responsiveness of a permissive parent with the highly structured expectations of authoritarian parents? You get a parent who sets limits, yet is kind. You get the authoritative parent, a style which psychologists acknowledge as the most effective for raising emotionally attached yet independent, successful, and mentally healthier, happy children. According to Diane Baumrind (Dewar, 2017):

Authoritative parents take a different, more moderate approach that emphasizes setting high standards, being nurturing and responsive, and showing respect for children as independent, rational beings. The authoritative parent expects maturity and cooperation, and offers children lots of emotional support.

The authoritative parent will provide their children with rules, and they will expect them to behave a certain way, but unlike authoritarian parents, they will make sure the children understand the reasons for those limits. They will also have age-appropriate expectations (you wouldn't demand the same attention span from a toddler as from a child that already attends school). They know that children should face the consequences of their actions, yet these consequences never imply taking away their love from them. These parents are also open to communication. They want to put themselves into their children's shoes.

Because they listen to their parents out of respect, and not out of fear, "there is even evidence that kids from authoritative homes are more attuned with their parents and less influenced by their peers" (Dewar, 2017). Children who grow up in these families tend to do better at school, they are generally well-behaved, and less prone to mental illness, addictions, or delinquency. They also tend to keep these strong, loving bonds with their parents way into adulthood, when they are already independent. And fortunately, they adopt the same style for raising their children as well.

Now that we have established the difference between the four parenting styles, you can probably guess that positive parenting falls not under the permissive style, but under the authoritative parenting instead: being firm, yet respectful and gentle. It sounds great but why is it so hard to achieve for many of us?

What Is Reactive Parenting?

Back to the time when Lanie was a toddler, I did my best to provide her with confidence and independence. I remember removing her bottle on her very first birthday, as the doctor had told me she was mature enough to drink from a sippy cup. By that time, Greg had taken a late shift, so he usually slept late in the morning. I was supposed to wake Lanie, give her some breakfast, and take her to daycare before setting off to work myself.

Most of the time, during her breakfast, she would spill the milk all over the table. Without my husband around to give me a helping hand, I was already in a hurry to get her to daycare and go to work. If I noticed she had poured some of the milk over her, that meant I had to dress her again, not to mention more load for our ever-growing pile of laundry... I felt frustrated and overwhelmed, so sometimes I scolded her while cleaning up the mess. While I was aware of the fact that Lanie wasn't doing it on purpose, it was just too much to handle.

The worst part was that, the more rushed I was, the more chances Lanie would spill the milk all over her clean clothes as well as the table, soaking her piece of toast, and making a big fuss about how she couldn't eat it wet. Things escalated quickly from this point, and our breakfast routine soon turned into a morning struggle! Of course, later I felt guilty and I apologized to Lanie, usually right before dropping her at daycare, which increased my feeling of guilt because I wouldn't get to see her until the afternoon.

I can understand now that back then, I was being a *reactive* parent: I got carried away from my emotions. Frustration for having to clean up, fear of being late—and thus, eventually losing my job—loneliness because my husband wasn't around, and I must admit, also some bitterness because I could hear him sound asleep in the bedroom, all of this piled up until I hit a spot in which my reaction was scolding a toddler for... being a toddler! While any parent can overreact or get carried away from time to time, if reactive parenting becomes a habit, it is hard to break and it encourages all kinds of negative behavior in children, especially as they get older. According to Dr. Lucy Russell (Russell, 2021):

[Recurrent reactive parenting] models a confrontational style of interacting which isn't always the best way for your child to communicate with others. Reactive parenting can contribute to feelings of shame or failure for you as a parent, and can leave your child feeling resentful or misunderstood, and producing their own negative responses.

While children are still toddlers, their way to escalate is usually through temper tantrums and fussiness. But if parents continue to surrender to their emotions and escalate, raising their children becomes a power struggle. Parents yell, they punish their children—in some cases, this even escalates into aggression—kids pull their strings to see how much they can get away with, and worst of all, they copy their parents' mechanism and lack self-regulation. Misbehaving, aggression, and oppositional behavior increment (Li, 2022). Altogether, the emotional bond between parents and children gets damaged.

Five Steps Towards Proactive Parenting

If you recognize some of the attributes of reacting parenting in yourself, know that it is up to you to break this circle. There are strategies you can start implementing today to change your reactiveness into proactiveness. Becoming a proactive parent means turning into a parent coach more than a parent cop (Richfield, 2019). That means don't let yourself get carried away by your emotions, understand the reasons behind your toddler's behavior, and act accordingly.

It is easier said than done, I know. But here are some basic tips that can help you become a proactive parent. It takes some time, consistency, and patience, but it is worth it, especially as your child gets older: "They will know right from wrong. They will choose the right thing because you have guided them in forming the correct habits and attitudes" (Mueller, 2012).

Parental Self-Discipline

Of course, it is hard to unlearn a parental habit you've kept for long, especially if you learned it during your childhood. If your parents used to react or overreact, you are probably copying the only parental mechanism you know! So taking a mental note of your negative reactions is the first step to overcoming them.

Every time you feel like screaming at your toddler, make a consistent effort to realize what is actually pulling your cords. Try to think for a second about how your little one means well, and that they are not doing whatever they are doing wrong on purpose. They don't want to piece you off, they are acting the way they are because they can't do otherwise. Temper tantrums are born out of the toddler's inability to recognize and handle their emotions: Sometimes they are tired or hungry, and other times they lack the words to express what's going on.

If you start seeing your toddler with loving eyes, you'll recognize them as little human beings that need guidance and direction, not little ungrateful brats that are doing anything out of their reach to punish mum or dad. "By thinking positively about your child, you will also act more compassionately, teaching your child to have empathy for others. Identify your triggers and their relationship to childhood" (Li, 2022).

Of course, you will lose your cool from time to time. You shouldn't attempt a complete transformation overnight because that way you'll only accumulate more frustration. Congratulate yourself if you can manage to low down your reactions at least some of the times: It's understandable if you lose your temper because your toddler threw your grandmother's favorite flower vase from the window, or because they tried to run away from you in a crowded place, but you can refrain from getting upset if they complain they are hungry after a long walk home. The best part is, the more you learn to control your impulses, the easier it will get.

Self-Care for Parents

Does your toddler strike your nerves simply by asking too many questions? Or by refusing to finish a meal? Are you questioning your parenting skills more often than not? Taking care of a child is hard! But before considering talking to a counselor, you might want to take a look at your daily routine: Are you getting enough sleep? Are your struggles during the meals keeping you from eating healthy yourself?

The truth is that unless you are well taken care of, you can't work well as a parent. You can't pour from an empty cup! So giving yourself some deserved time is basic if you want to become a proactive parent. You need to sleep enough hours every night—well, most of the nights at least—you need to eat well, and you need to make some time during the day to do something you enjoy (Li, 2022):

You don't have to take on a long-term goal like "be healthy" which can be daunting. Start with small steps. Listen to one song, read one chapter in your favorite book, or take a short walk to the mailbox. No matter how busy you are, set aside time to do something that helps you relax. Make it a part of your parenting routine.

It may be hard to find the time, especially if you work outside your home and your toddler attends daycare. Guilt and social pressure to *be there for them* make it difficult to schedule a date night with your significant other, or drinks with friends. But you should do it anyway: If not every week, at least every other week, or once a month. You need some time to put the mum or the dad aside, and simply be *you*. It will be good for your child as well!

Physical, Mental, and Emotional Health of the Parent

If your toddler feels bad, you probably rush to the emergency room, or at least get an appointment or a video call with their pediatrician, right? Unfortunately, parents usually neglect their own health. How many times have you gotten out of bed to make breakfast although you had some temperature? Again, if you are unwell, first of all, you need to take care of yourself. Make your physical well-being a priority! Don't be afraid to ask for help, and accept any you can get.

The same applies to your mental and emotional well-being. If you wouldn't wait to fix a broken bone, why do you delay going to therapy if you are still struggling with anxiety, or maybe are facing the consequences of long-time sleep deprivation? Particularly in the case of new mums (but not exclusively), postpartum depression symptoms can emerge even after a year after giving birth (Mayo Clinic, 2018). Possible symptoms include reduced interest in activities you enjoyed before, irritability, feelings of worthlessness, or believing you are not a good parent. Untreated, postpartum depression can last for months, or even longer, and can lead to more severe symptoms that include suicidal thoughts or panic attacks. If you relate to some of these symptoms, don't wait any longer: Call your doctor, and get the necessary treatment.

Overcoming Mom Guilt

Society sells us motherhood as an ideal state: In advertising, movies, books, and nowadays social media, we all see those perfect pictures of beautiful mums walking in a park, holding their little one's hand, peacefully staring at a butterfly, or their kids jumping on a pile of autumn leaves with a big smile on their face. We see sculpted-body mums coming back from the gym with enough time to grow organic vegetables in their backyards and cook a healthy lunch for a family of five, every child eating up to the last bite of their plates. We are exposed to spotless birthday parties where children open presents and cheer in joy.

But this is a fake world! You live in an actual family, with a real toddler that refuses to keep walking in the park and wants to be carried, no matter that you are holding two grocery bags and they already weigh 40 pounds. It's a world in which you rush from the office and you pick up your child late from daycare, and for dinner, they have to settle with a microwave meal because you didn't have the time to go to the supermarket, least of all cooking, and they dislike that meal because "it tastes funny." Their birthday parties are messy, and by the end of the afternoon, they may get upset because they got a *red* Transformer, and not the blue one they wanted so bad!

I release you from the guilt, you fellow mum! You are not a bad mother for hating high-energy toddlers. It's okay if you can't stand other children, and it's okay too if sometimes you can't stand your own! The truth is you can't lower your guard for a second. Toddlers are a risk for material objects, pets, others, as well as for themselves. Not to mention that constant tantrums make it hard to enjoy parenthood.

Becoming part of a mum tribe (whether online or in your local playground, for example) can help you vent and overcome some of the difficulties of being a parent. The only thing you have to watch out for is mom-shaming, which has become increasingly common because of social media exposure. Everybody has something to say about your choices as a parent, and no single decision will make them completely happy. But this doesn't matter as long as it works with your family.

Becoming a Zen Parent

While it's okay to not be okay with toddler terror, you should also keep in mind that this too shall pass. Staying calm in the chaos is hard, but understanding the real reasons why your toddler acts the way they act may help you raise your tolerance. They are not misbehaving on purpose, they are not pushing your cords, and they are not trying to test you. They are simply young children who still lack some emotional skills. If you understand this, you can develop a method to avoid heating up and thus, turning back to reacting (Richfield, 2019):

Accept that these behaviors are part of everyone's parenting journey and not a reason to become an overheated parent. Develop a three-step plan to follow when a hot-spot is spotted: A for awareness, B for breathe deeply, and C for calmly respond.

The good part is, once you unlearn reactive parenting and you manage to keep calm most of the time, your child will learn to copy that mechanism and, in time, develop their own impulse control. This way, being a proactive parent becomes easier later on. You'll thank it once they hit puberty! "No matter how much effort this seems to take at first, later childhood discipline will be much easier and your child will learn to do the right thing calmly in the face of frustration" (Mueller, 2012).

Chapter Takeaways

- Most of what you learned about parenting, you learned by the way your parents raised you back when you were a child.

- Our parents' generation was generally not aware of the benefits of positive parenting, and that's why most of them didn't raise us following its principles.

- Adopting positive parenting means, in many ways, unlearning the parenting style you willingly or subconsciously adopted.

- Many people mistake positive parenting for being permissive. But unlike this parenting style, positive parenting implies being firm and setting clear rules. This way, when it comes to the four parenting styles defined by Diana Baumrind—authoritarian, permissive, neglective, and authoritative—positive parenting relates with the fourth: This means combining high responsiveness with highly structured expectations.

- Adopting a positive parenting style also needs unlearning reactive parenting: This means, getting easily carried away by your emotions and reacting, or overreacting, to your child's behavior.

- The first steps into achieving a positive parenting style you can implement today are working on your self-discipline, adopting habits of personal care, taking care both of your physical and mental well-being, overcoming guilt, and accepting your child the way they are.

- By becoming responsive instead of reactive, you create stronger bonds with your child, and you also teach them throughout the example how to learn self-control from an early age. Positive parenting takes an effort, but it will definitely pay off!

In the next chapter, we will talk about understanding toddlerhood and challenging behaviors. As we have seen, this will help you improve your parenting style, lowering your reactiveness and anticipating difficult situations before they happen.

Chapter 2

Putting Yourself in Their Little Shoes

The Golden Rule of Parenting is do unto your children as you wish your parents had done unto you! –Louise Hart

Back in July 2016, a little boy and his father were together celebrating Grandma's 90th birthday. Something, most likely a helicopter, caught the eye of young George, who had turned three some days prior. His dad crouched down to talk to him, looking him straight in the eye, and responding to his son with a loving gesture. This caused some distress to George's great-grandmother, who discreetly scolded her grandson, telling him to get up. Many cameras caught the moment, and the news hit social media around the world.

Does it surprise you? Maybe I should tell you by now that the little boy in the story was Prince George of Wales, his father was Prince William, then second-in-line to the British Crown, and the upset grandmother was Queen Elizabeth herself, who thought—not without a reason—that her grandson was breaking the royal protocol by kneeling in public during the Royal Air Force display that was taken place at that time (Mulroy, 2016). News portals from Great Britain and other parts of the world reproduced the story.

This would not be the last time Prince William put his children's interests in front of his royal duties, and ever since, he has been spotted crouching or bending over whenever he needs to address one of his three kids. He doesn't do it to upset his elders, but he's following a technique known as "active listening," one of the principles of positive parenting we will go through in this chapter. Prince William and his wife, Princess Catherine, have received some criticism, but also all sorts of praise for their parenting style. Fortunately for all of us, we don't need to break any protocols when we put into practice active listening or any of the many tips we'll discuss!

Why does your precious little baby turn into a creature from outer space within a matter of weeks? Why do they have so little patience? How come they don't talk, yet manage to say 'no' to every single one of your requests? Are they *trying* to drive you mad? In this chapter, I will try to provide some answers to these common questions every parent has.

We'll begin by defining *toddlers*, and what makes them different from babies and preschoolers. Only by understanding them can we approach their challenging behaviors without boiling up and turning to reactive parenting. We'll also explore some ways of connecting to them—as Prince William does!—how to communicate with them even before they can talk, and how the principles of positive parenting replace punishments while still aiming for discipline.

Why Do We Call Them "Toddlers"?

The basic definition of 'toddler' is "a person who toddles," and if you have never used the verb "to toddle" you are not alone! It means to move in short steps, usually unsteady, and that's why it has become a synonym for children aged one to three years old. About the time they reach their first birthday, some babies are learning to stand up and walk unsteadily—hence the term. However, when it comes to milestones, you should keep in mind that every child is different, and they don't achieve the same results at the same time. While some 12-month-olds are already walking, some others won't do it until they are 18 months old. In case you have questions about your child's development, you should always check with your pediatrician.

A toddler is different from a baby because they have gained a whole new world with their new motor skills: They no longer depend on being carried (of course they still *want* to be carried, especially when mummy is tired and her back is killing her!), they can move around, and they have a fascinating world to discover at their feet! Walking is only the beginning! "As she grows, your toddler will begin to walk alone, run, and engage in physical activity with objects, such as pulling a toy behind her or kicking a ball" (Phillips, 2014).

Of course, deep down they are still helpless, and unlike newborns, who spend most of their time asleep, they need constant supervision: You can no longer rely on the baby monitor! There is furniture to climb, windows to open, pets to chase, poisonous substances that look yummy... Even the sweetest, kindest toddler (is there such a thing?) will keep your hands full only for keeping them safe!

Also, a toddler is different from a preschooler because they have yet to learn to talk (although some babies start producing their first words by the time they turn one, or even sooner). While some toddlers display the first signs of being able to potty train around 18-24 months, for most of them it may take months to be fully prepared to get rid of the diapers. And changing several times a day the diapers of a two-year-old is not the same as changing a baby! Toddlers may resist diaper change, and—because they are already eating solid foods as most of their calorie intake—boy, those things can stink! Most important, a toddler's brain is still developing in the sense of recognizing their emotions and regulating self-control. A well-educated preschooler can understand reasons, but a young toddler can't!

So, there you go! Mix the frequent needs of a baby (long hours of sleep, frequent feedings, the need for diapers, the lack of structured language to communicate, their complete inability to calculate risks) together with the freedom of movement and the urge to explore, and BAM! You get that explosive cocktail of emotions, actions, and headaches for the parents that toddlers are.

However, I don't want you to stay with this picture for long. A toddler is not only a misbehaving big baby, no. A toddler is also a source of fun, curiosity, marvel, gratitude, and infinite doses of love. The more you understand them, the more you'll appreciate them and enjoy this stage of your child's life that, like any other stage, is temporary.

I get you when you say you are tired: I have raised my firstborn with many difficulties during her toddlerhood, and now I'm dealing with three-year-old twins, and they have their good days as well as their bad ones! I can't push you to enjoy your toddler, but if you acquire some positive parenting skills, you'll find out you will! Well, at least most of the time.

Connecting Before Correcting

I already mentioned that positive parenting, following Dr. Adler's discoveries, considers every child as inherently good. Behind each problematic behavior, there are reasons other than "they are just pulling your strings." Your toddler doesn't run away from you in the playground because they don't love you anymore. They don't refuse to finish their broccoli to make you mad. They are displaying a new sense of self, achieving new independence, and trying to show you so.

Some parents experience suffering in secret—together with a pang of huge guilt—because they think they have lost their little baby, and this causes them even more trouble to positively engage with their toddler at this new stage of their lives. Look at your child with loving eyes: They are the same person they have always been, only that they have grown and are acquiring new skills. And all of this is because you did a great job as a parent! Let's keep in mind every parent's purpose when it comes to their children in providing the appropriate tools to turn them into functional adults, for them to find a place in society. To achieve that, they have to take baby steps (pun intended!).

And here's something you might not have considered yet: Your toddler is struggling too. While they adore their new mobility and independence, it also scares them big time. They need frequent comfort and reassurance. They want you to put them down and let them explore the world, but at the same time, they need to be certain they can still go back to your safe hug if they find something they don't like.

Most of the time, when a toddler displays problematic behavior, they are trying to catch your attention. They need reassurance that no matter what, you are still there for them, and you still love them. That's why it is so important at this age to remain positive and to keep engaging in verbal praise and physical contact. Give them a lot of kisses, and tell them that you love them every day, as many times a day as possible (particularly at those times you don't feel like saying it). Remind yourself that they are not little monsters but little children struggling to learn, and sometimes they feel inadequate because the world is not made at their size and shape.

PUTTING YOURSELF IN THEIR LITTLE...

If you are exhausted after a long day of preparing meals, going back and forth carrying an already heavy stroller with a toddler that whines when sitting down but also refuses to walk in the intended direction, you may faint into your bed at night and wonder when you have the time to emotionally connect with your child. And still, I cannot emphasize enough how a healthy, emotional connection is basic if you want your toddler to accept some basic ground rules and slowly change their behavior to match your (and society's) expectations.

Author Pam Leo describes this emotional connection as filling your child's "love cup." In her book *Connection Parenting*, she suggests every child should spend at least 10 minutes a day with an adult that grants them their undivided attention and affection. If there is more than one adult that can do this, the better. But your toddler needs "at least one person in their life who thinks the sun rises and sets on them, someone who delights in their existence" (Leo, 2007). You don't need to be around your toddler 24/7 to display unconditional love, as long as you provide them with these daily brief times of play, attachment, and enjoying your time together.

In further chapters, we will explore some of the ways you can spend these daily 10 minutes. Kelly Holmes, from *Happy You Happy Family*, suggests, among other strategies, reading your toddler a book, saying positive phrases, playing with your toddler (or simply being there while they play, engaging as much or as little as they request), and putting down your cellphone during those precious minutes of emotional connection (Holmes, 2016).

A long, significant hug releases serotonin, it helps your child and yourself relax, feels calmer, protected, and in a better mood! Holmes advises you to "make sure it's a good quality hug of six seconds or more" (Holmes, 2016), and don't just get into the habit of giving them a quick pat on the back. Besides, the same way we quickly lose the habit of maintaining healthy physical contact with our children as they grow up, if we get used to hugging each other every day, this can become part of our routine as well! And teenagers and adults alike benefit from healthy physical contact with a loving parent.

You may believe you are already fulfilling your child's need to play by taking them to the ballpark, the playground, the zoo, or providing them with expensive toys, but what they cherish the most is your time (Lively, 2014):

If you want to really connect with your kids, I learned that it's not enough to just take them to the playground and watch them, you need to play with them (that's the engagement part)! Although it can feel tiresome to play with your kids after a long day, the benefits far outweigh the negatives.

It takes some time, consistency, and effort. But only after you have set the foundations of a loving, emotional connection with your child, will you be able to implement the principles of positive parenting for setting boundaries and dealing with problematic behavior effectively. Besides, once you get used to those precious interactions, you won't only discover your toddler displays less mischief and becomes more cooperative, you'll find out you actually can enjoy spending some time with the little monster!

How to Communicate With Your Toddler

It's funny how we didn't have communication issues back then when our child was a baby and suddenly, now that they have turned into toddlers, we expect them to listen up and to do as we say. Maybe it's because when they were babies, we were used to them not being able to talk. However, just because a child turns one and starts uttering their first words (*mummy, daddy, water, more*) they don't turn into competent speakers! And they won't be, at least for a couple more years.

Yet, toddlers understand a lot of what we say to them. So we have to watch our language, something we should have done from the time they were born; however, a baby won't repeat a curse in front of your mother-in-law and point at you when the lady demands to know where they learned such a nasty thing. Positive parenting encourages open, constant communication with children of all ages. Here are a few tips you can start implementing right away without any effort.

Speak About What You Do

"Now, I'm taking off your pajamas and putting on your t-shirt." "I'm mixing the eggs with the milk so I can pour them into this pan, see?" "We are getting in the car so mummy can drive you to daycare." Labeling your actions is a great way of later anticipating them for your toddler. Their little brains are absorbing language as if they were sponges, so soon they'll be able to relate each word or phrase with a concept, a process, or a situation. By the way, this is something parents are encouraged to do from day one with their babies, but if you haven't done it so far, toddlerhood is a great moment to start.

Make Sure You Are at Their Reach

Remember that story about Prince William and his little boy? Crouching down is a great way of guaranteeing your toddler pays attention to what you say. You literally stand at their height! Your body language states that you are listening way more than a single "Sure, you can talk to me!" Look at them straight in the eye, use a kind, soft tone of voice, and talk to them.

It goes the other way around as well: If your toddler is attempting to communicate, if they are saying words or asking you a question, active listening shows them you really care for what they have to say. No matter if Her Royal Majesty has some complaints about the lack of protocols! Try not to interrupt your child, or fill in the blanks by completing a sentence. Instead, actively engage in conversation by adding expressions such as "that's interesting!" or "really?" They do a lot in showing your toddler you care about what they have to say.

If you practice active listening, your toddler will also learn by copying you, so in time they will learn to wait for their turn to speak, don't interrupt when others are talking, and show interest in what you have to say as well.

Understand Them Beyond Words

Some parents become concerned when their toddlers aren't speaking by a certain age. Sure, some charts state that by their first birthday they should already be pronouncing their first identifiable word, by 18 months they should have incremented their vocabulary and be able to answer 'yes' and 'no' at least with gestures... Again, each child is unique and they all have their own pace when it comes to development. Instead of looking at the charts, you should talk to your pediatrician if you are concerned about a possible delay in speech development. Chances are they are normal, healthy toddlers, but if there is any problem, it should be addressed as soon as possible for better results.

In case everything is fine, and you are only getting anxious about properly understanding them, you should try to find other methods of communication your toddler is already implementing: "Is he doing a lot of pointing, head-nodding, or grunting in a certain direction? Toddlers develop ways to get their point across even without using words" (Phillips, 2014).

Repeat and Add One

Toddlers can get easily frustrated when they find out something is beyond their reach. This could be pulling the dog's ears, eating chocolate instead of their veggies, crossing the street without holding your hand, or getting the most expensive toy in the toy store. It also applies to their physical or cognitive abilities: A toddler can get so angry because they can't pile the blocks that they start throwing them all over their bedroom! When it comes to language, correcting their pronunciation before they are mature enough to articulate certain sounds may be counterproductive.

Instead of correcting them, try repeating what they said to show them you understood (not mimicking their imperfect pronunciation, of course!). If your toddler says "*tuck*," you answer "that's right, it's a *truck!*" But, also to increase their vocabulary, you can try repeating their words and adding an extra: "that's right, it's a *big truck!*" (Kennedy, 2020)

Naming the Emotions

Part of putting yourself in your toddler's shoes is understanding their emotions. Even if something isn't a big deal for you (such as the ice cream store running out of sprinkles), "remember that to them, this is a big deal—just as things like work or finances are stressful for you" (Kennedy, 2020). While you mustn't tolerate certain behaviors, you have to accept every emotion, and teach your toddler that it's okay to feel that way:

- "You are frustrated because there are no sprinkles, I understand. I want sprinkles too, but we can have them some other time. We can still eat chocolate ice cream once you stop crying."

- "You are sad because your car lost one of its wheels. We don't throw toys because they could hurt us or another person. You can still play with the car by letting it down the slide, or you can choose another car from your box of toys."

- "You are angry with your big sister because she ate the last cookie. But you also used a very ugly word. We only say kind things to one another. Besides, look! She feels ashamed about not sharing the cookie."

- "You are hungry and tired from spending all that time in the mall. You will have some nice strawberries and fresh water as soon as we get home. It will be faster if you stand up and walk with me to the car."

Using Positive Statements

Children—and anyone else, actually!—respond better when stated affirmations instead of denials. So a good strategy for communicating with a toddler is turning your NOs into positive statements. Sure, you will yell "DON'T touch that stove!" once in a while. But try to keep your phrases positive when the situation allows you to reformulate them.

- "Be nice to your baby sister. Touch her gently!" is better than "don't hit your sister."

- "Use a quiet voice here so I can understand you" is better than "don't yell!"

- "You can caress the puppy, he likes it this way" (while showing) is better than "Don't pull his tail or else he'll bite you."

- "This is Mark's dinosaur. You can play with this other red one" is better than "Don't take other kid's toys!"

One exception to the rule is irony. Children don't get it until they are preteens. So don't try to get them to understand if you use it when they are misbehaving. "Sure! You'll watch TV now that you are being soooo patient," with a contemptuous look won't get your toddler to stop nagging for their favorite show. Instead, you'll just confound them.

Punishing vs. Empowering

Positive parenting makes a strong focus on disciplining children. We all need to learn to play by the rules if we want to become an active, productive part of society (whether that society is a kindergarten class, a girl-scout group, or an international company). And children learn the rules through observation as well as through someone teaching them. What they see you do matters way more than what you tell them to do! If you tell your toddler to "throw the candy wrap in a paper basket" but you often litter when you go to the playground, guess what? They'll just do as they see! The same applies to any other example, from obeying traffic lights to treating people with kindness and respect.

When you practice positive parenting, you will not let your toddler do as they please, as some permissive parents do, because you understand that this is not good for them. But you won't force random rules on them either, as authoritarian parents do. Instead, you try to teach them why they should follow a certain norm.

- "We wash our hands before lunch because otherwise, we could get sick."

- "You should pick your toys after playing so tomorrow you'll find them in their spot right away and you'll have more time to have fun."

- "We walk when we are in the supermarket because it's crowded, and you could get hurt if you bump into another person's shopping cart."

Does this mean your toddler will start behaving properly? No! Of course, since they are still learning the rules, you'll need to remind them often until they get them right. But even then, every toddler misbehaves from time to time. Your duty as a responsible parent is to understand that this is not something they do on purpose. Sometimes, they are tired, or hungry, and some other times they just want some attention from you. In the past, they have learned that whatever you are doing, you stop doing it and you run to them if they, let's say, attempt to climb the coffee table. That's why they keep doing it when you are busy helping their older sibling do their homework, cooking dinner, or—God forbids!—staring at your phone for more than five minutes. Amy McCready, founder of Positive Parenting Solutions and expert in discipline, "suggests stopping bad behavior by addressing a toddler's need for both emotional connection and power" (Phillips, 2014).

If you punish a toddler for their bad behavior, they will get the attention they were looking for. But they won't learn from what they have done. This could lead them to repeat such negative behavior in the future or, eventually, make sure you don't find out about what they did! They will try to behave properly at your sight because they fear you, not because they respect you or understand you. This is what happens if you are an authoritarian parent imposing a disproportionate punishment, or a reactive parent yelling at them.

Instead, positive parenting focuses on correcting the behavior in ways different than punishment.

Distracting

Distract the toddler, and get them out of the situation without yelling or scolding them. If you are busy in the kitchen, ask them to help you mix the sugar and the flour or count the spoons; or whatever keeps them busy and in plain sight. Be careful the stove isn't currently on! Never have hot stuff near a toddler.

Giving Options

Give the toddler options to show them they keep some degree of control, like in this scenario: "You have to get down from that table and I still need to help your sister with her homework. Do you want to join us and paint a nice picture while we work? Or would you rather bring some blocks and play nearby?"

Correcting Them in Private

While a public scolding—whether in the waiting lodge in a crowded airport or at a family dinner—can humiliate the toddler, a private correction teaches them what's expected behavior. If you give your toddler a lecture in front of other people and everyone looks at them, they become ashamed and they learn to avoid a certain behavior because it could get them into trouble, but not because it's wrong. On the contrary, if you take your toddler to a private place and you communicate with them, they will listen to your reasons and they will eventually learn from their mistakes.

Fixing It Up

If your toddler's misbehaving has consequences, they should try to make amends. Going back to that time I used to get mad at Lanie for spilling her cup, I eventually taught her how to use a kitchen rag and help me "clean." Sure, being a toddler, she created even more mess and I had to clean up after her anyway, but at least she learned her actions had a consequence. Eventually, she learned to be more careful when drinking from her cup.

Chapter Takeaways

- Toddlers are different from babies because they have acquired a lot of skills. They are energetic, curious, restless, and always willing to go one step further in their learning process. Yet, they lack the self-control of older children. That's why they are such a handful!

- Understanding why your toddler behaves the way they do, knowing that they are struggling too, and that they need your loving reassurance more than ever is the best way to learn parental self-control and avoid reacting.

- Before correcting your toddler's behavior, you need to connect with them. This means providing them with a lot of positive interactions, physical touch, kind phrases, and spending quality one-on-one time with them every day.

- Before your toddler can learn to speak properly, they still understand you. Some strategies to communicate with them include, but are not limited to: labeling your actions, practicing active listening, making an effort to understand their body language and signals, using positive statements, and naming their emotions.

- Toddlers learn the rules by copying you more than by listening to you. Teach with an example!

- Positive parenting disciplines children, not through punishment but by teaching them the reasons for the given rules and the consequences of their actions instead.

What if your toddler doesn't understand the reasons? Are you exasperated after dealing with yet another bedtime tantrum? That's okay. In the following chapter, we will further explore tips and strategies positive parenting implements for managing bad behaviors.

Chapter 3

Teaching, Not Taming!

Are we parenting the whole human being or are we just on Behavior Patrol? Because I can tell you from experience that when we operate as Behavior Patrol, we miss a whole lot about the human being. –Rebecca Eanes

Picture this: You are going to the greengrocer's with your two-year-old. He's tired after a long afternoon in the park, and you have picked him up for the past two blocks, but now you need to put him down to get some vegetables for dinner. As soon as he stands on the floor, he runs towards a box of tomatoes yelling "Balls, balls!" and he reaches for the largest one. You kindly take the tomato out of his hand just in time to avoid a huge disaster, but you can't prevent the consequent meltdown. Your toddler starts to cry and yell. You know he doesn't even like tomatoes! People are staring at you. As he escalates, you consider one of the following:

- Leave the greengrocer's without buying anything, and set up for some frozen beans instead.

- Scolding your toddler and apologizing to everyone around you as he keeps crying. Do your shopping as fast as possible and drag away your weeping monster as if chased by the devil.

- Giving him back the tomato, hoping he doesn't smash it on the floor.

- Kindly explain to your toddler you won't buy tomatoes because he doesn't eat them, but he can pick a carrot or a banana.

What would a mum who practices positive parenting do? If you think the answer is D, you still have some things to learn about toddlerhood (by the way, that was my first pick too!).

Why are toddlers so hard to comfort sometimes? How can we get them out of a temper tantrum? How does positive parenting handle challenging behaviors, such as reluctance to go to sleep, being rude to their parents, fighting with their siblings or playmates, or turning 'no' into their favorite (and single) response for any request? In this chapter, we'll see how to manage some typical situations, and what kind of discipline better works for a toddler.

Some Basic Lines to Follow

You should always keep in mind that your toddler's behavior has a reason. They aren't *being naughty* or *pulling your strings*. Most likely, they are trying to attract your attention, they haven't learned the difference between right and wrong, or they are overcome by an emotion they can't identify or express.

Positive parents are consistent and reliable in their discipline methods. They set realistic goals, make their expectations clear, try to understand their children, and display affection and appreciation (Kennedy, 2020). This means that instead of punishing a child if they misbehave, they'll attempt to prevent the undesired behavior first. You do this by anticipating the situation and the possible ways your toddler may react based on how they are feeling.

You set boundaries that are clear and age-appropriate, but at the same time, you explain to your child the reason for that limit. Even a toddler can understand the reason for some basic instructions if you use appropriate language: "We don't pick tomatoes from the box because if they fall, the floor will get dirty. We wait for that man to hand them to us instead." If you start a big speech about the importance of washing their hands after coming back from the park and handling edibles, or that tomatoes are fragile and because his fine motors are still developing, you would have to pay for all of the ones he breaks, it would be as effective as having him sit through a college lecture on local agriculture!

As for temper tantrums, they put your toddler in a place where they are no longer in control. They can't understand reasons or change their behavior based on punishments and sometimes not even rewards will work. Toddlers get carried away by their emotions, and they need you to keep your cool and help them get over the situation. If you are anything like me, you find regular temper tantrums the worst part of having a toddler! That's why we'll start approaching this problematic behavior first.

Dealing With Temper Tantrums

Every two-year-old has a meltdown now and then. It happens when they are experiencing an emotion that overpasses them. They can't identify the feeling, they can't talk about what's wrong, and the mixture of that frustration together with the original emotion becomes an explosive cocktail. They are more common among children who still lack verbal skills. So tantrums tend to spread out and become less frequent as the child acquires some tools, both verbal and emotional.

An occasional temper tantrum is part of normal toddlerhood! "These young kids have big emotions but cannot express them in words. They also don't have the ability to regulate themselves because that part of the brain is not yet developed" (Li, 2022). The problem is that this undesired explosion can become a regular pattern if you don't address it properly. It's your job as a parent to teach toddlers how to self-regulate.

And if you don't, that's how you get children that still throw temper tantrums when they are in elementary school, much to their teacher's and their classmates' shock. And you may agree with me that it's one thing to see a toddler getting upset because they won't get off the swing, and another different thing is seeing a seven-year-old breaking their homework in pieces because the teacher graded it with a B.

Public Temper Tantrums

Some parents feel discouraged, judged, or unable to manage the situation when their children have a tantrum in a public place. If we understand that tantrums are a normal behavior of toddlers, then you shouldn't feel judged because your toddler is being a toddler in the first place!

When your child is experiencing a temper tantrum, try to identify what's going on in the first place: "You are upset because you had a great time on the swings and now it's time to go." You can't reason with them in the heart of the storm, but sometimes, putting into words whatever detonates the behavior can help them calm down. "Remember: Toddlers often struggle to regulate their emotions and learn by testing limits. Acknowledging their feelings (even if you don't fully understand them) tells your toddler that you hear them" (Scher, 2022). This provides validation to their emotions.

If your toddler whines or cries, this doesn't necessarily mean you have to correct them. Understanding their emotions also means letting them express themselves. "An acknowledged child can move on without the need to misbehave. They may still be grumpy, but they do not need to act out to get heard" (Li, 2022). Again, you can help them put their feelings into words: "You are sad now, I understand, and it's okay to cry. But we can come back to the park tomorrow, I bet it will be a nice, sunny day!" If a toddler yells, don't yell louder. You can tell them to use a softer tone of voice instead.

Sometimes, the tantrum won't go away, and this can be specifically difficult to manage if done in public. Some parents give up, and let the child spend more time in the swing (even if there is a line of children waiting to use it). But this only teaches the toddler that this behavior pays off! Other parents scold or humiliate their child: Although this could put an end to the tantrum, it does work for the wrong reasons. Basically, you scare your child. But they won't learn to manage their emotions through fear, and temper tantrums will repeat. "Often, unnatural negative consequences cannot stop bad behavior, nor does it teach good ones" (Li, 2022).

What *should* you do, then? Your job is to be a captain in the middle of a storm. You hold the rudder tight, and you keep the ship from crashing into the rocks! In other words, control that nobody (or nothing) gets damaged, first of all, your toddler. Hold them tight, firm, yet kindly, to refrain them from pulling their hair (or another child's!) or banging themselves against a wall. Don't allow them to push you or hit you. Keep holding them without yelling. Your voice tone should remain kind. Once the tantrum starts to fade, only then you can go back to addressing the behavior: "Being upset is okay, screaming and kicking it's not."

Later, when your toddler has calmed down, reassure them that you love them, but you can't allow that behavior. Don't punish them for the tantrum! They are too young to relate something that passed several minutes ago (ages!) with your current anger. Kindly explain to them the consequences of their actions: "You love being on the swings, but other children want to play on them as well. You have to accept getting off the swing if you want to go back to the playground tomorrow."

You can prevent some tantrums if you anticipate your toddler's behavior. In the given example, you can create anticipation in different moments:

- Before you go to the park: "Remember what happened last time. You can play on the swings if you want to, but you have to get down when I tell you to."

- Before you sit them in the swing: "Great, have fun at the swing! Just remember other children are waiting to use them too."

- Before you get them down: "Okay, now three more pushes and we get down."

Another way to deal with some tantrums is distracting your toddler from whatever is causing them to get upset: "Hey! Look at that slide! It looks fun, let's try it before we go home, shall we?" Most toddlers get temper tantrums when they are tired or hungry. You can also anticipate these situations: Bring a healthy snack to the park, or take them home before they are overtired.

With older toddlers, you may get stubbornness instead of raging tantrums: "No, I don't want to go home, I want to stay on the swings!" If anticipating didn't work, you can try negotiating with them: "I know, but that little girl wants to use the swing now, I bet it would be fun taking turns and pushing her. Later, she can push you!" And if negotiation doesn't work, firmly yet kindly you have to set your foot down. Taking them off the swing, in this scenario, will not be a punishment, but a direct consequence of their actions: "The playground is not yours, but it belongs to every child. We'll come back to play when you decide you are ready to share it. In the meantime, you can play with your toys."

Mealtime Tantrums

Oh, the mealtimes… The perfect family moment for sitting together and talking about our day while we enjoy a delicious and healthy homemade dinner. That is unless you have a toddler who refuses to eat no matter what. Mealtimes can become battlefields especially since there are dangerous weapons at your toddler's reach! Here, we will see some of the common sceneries and how to address them.

Sometimes, mealtime tantrums happen because, paradoxically, your toddler is *really* hungry! They may start to cry and refuse to eat their spaghetti because they are too hot, and this causes frustration together with hunger escalates into… you've guessed it, right? Yes, another tantrum! Addressing their feelings can help them overcome these impatient and powerless sensations: "I know it's hard to wait for your spaghetti to cool down, right? In the meantime, I'll grill some cheese on it. Why don't you take a sip of water?" If they get impatient, a timer can help them better keep track—the same when the meal is not ready yet. Giving them age-appropriate chores to do (like bending the paper napkins or setting the spoons next to the plates, never handling hot food or sharp objects) can also help them regain control and keep the tantrum away altogether.

At the same time, sometimes toddlers refuse to eat because they are not hungry or because they don't like the food—or they straight won't try it! In any case, never force them to eat if they refuse, but don't compensate later with snacks, especially sweets. Amy McCready, from *Positive Parenting Solutions*, suggests that sending a child to sleep without having dinner is not a punishment, but a natural consequence of their decisions: "Make your child's eating habits their responsibility, not yours. Remember, you can't "make" your kids eat-no matter how hard you try! Your job is to prepare a healthy meal. Your child's job is to eat it or not" (McCready, 2015). Other ways you can approach picky eaters are:

- Let them become involved in the selection, shopping, and even preparation of meals. We have seen how this creates in toddlers the so-much-desired sense of control!

- You don't have time to make a different dish for each family member, but you can still try to give them some choices: For example, some children like carrots but don't like green peas. Don't try to force the vegetable they dislike by "mixing it up." Instead, you can serve them in separate bowls so that everyone can choose their side dish.

- Don't label your child as a "bad eater," nor as a "good eater" because in this way, their siblings will be labeled in comparison. Avoid statements such as "She will never eat that!" or "He hates vegetables." They will only reinforce negative behaviors.

- If you are preparing a dish for the first time and you are pretty sure they won't try it, you can reduce the struggle by adding some healthy food you know they like: "Offer at least one healthy item your child is sure to like at every sitting" (McCready, 2015).

- Remember that your toddler learns more from watching you than from listening to you: If you eat healthily and are willing to try new things, sooner or later they'll start incorporating new foods into their diet. Offer them, just don't force them.

I know that letting them eat while they watch their favorite cartoon may seem a solution since they are distracted and you can sneak the spoonful of cauliflower puree before they can realize what's going on. But first, the same as you can't force a child into eating, you shouldn't trick them either: You are only creating more ground for a battlefield! And second, although we are all busy and sometimes it's easier to let them dine in front of the TV set or while playing with their tablets, sharing a meal can be so much more! It's the perfect time for practicing connection with your toddler. Focus on their expressions so they can see you are actively engaged in communicating, talking to them, singing a song, and smiling... instead of displaying anxiety because they don't eat as much or as well as you think they should be eating. If you do so, they'll feel better predisposed towards the food on their plate, as they won't need to use it as a means to get your attention: They already got it for all the good reasons!

Bedtime Tantrums

Another common situation when toddlers get out of control is their time for bed. How can you avoid bad behavior and struggles at bedtime? The first thing I suggest you do is to prevent them in the first place by creating a consistent and predictable bedtime routine. After dinner, allow your children to relax: No more screen time, only quiet activities such as reading or coloring. Give them a relaxing, warm bath, put them in their pajamas, brush their teeth, let them choose a bedtime story (or two, or three), sing them a lullaby, and maybe let them have one last sip of water. And then, the fun is over and it's time to go to sleep. A bedtime chart with pictures can help them understand these steps and know what to look forward to.

Remember that positive parenting is focused on rewarding instead of punishing. If your child refuses to go to bed, a consistent bedtime routine can help them understand the consequences of their actions: "Because you took so long to brush your teeth, now there is not enough time for a second story. Hopefully, tomorrow we'll do it faster!"

Most toddlers refuse to go to sleep at the requested time for many reasons, such as:

- They are not yet tired, or they are overtired.
- They are tired, yet they want to do something way more exciting than going to sleep.
- They don't like being alone in their bedroom, and because they are already too big for their cribs, they refuse to stay in bed.
- They want to call your attention.

Let's address the common reasons listed above and suggest some solutions.

Find The Appropriate Bedtime

Sometimes, our family routines don't match the toddler's natural circadian rhythm. As you may have noticed, putting in bed a child that isn't yet tired, or that is overtired, can result in a bedtime tantrum. There is a gentle sleep training method known as the fading method, that focuses on taking notes of the times of the day in which your child falls asleep easily. Once you have tracked their natural rhythm, you can slowly make adjustments to the routine and move it forward (or delay it a little) to better match your toddler's natural sleeping time (Geddes, 2022).

If they aren't tired at night, perhaps you should reduce their nap time.

Reduce Nighttime Stimulus

Watching TV or playing with your cell phone in the evening has negative effects on your toddler's bedtime routine. An hour before bed, they should not be exposed to screens, the lights in the house should be dim, and the sounds quieter. If the child is too engaged with exciting activities, they will resist bedtime and have trouble falling—or staying—asleep.

Create a Cozy Atmosphere

You can't expect a toddler to embrace their bedtime routine and willingly go to bed if they are having a bad time. Try to empathize with your child: Are they afraid of the dark? You can leave a nightlight on. Do they need a special stuffed animal as a company? This is normal, and it can be handy for dealing with bedtime problems. Just make sure you have a secret spare one hidden in the back of your closet, in case their special friend goes missing!

Give Them Attention (But Not Intervention)

Toddlers may get out of bed 20 times in a row if they find out this is a way to get their parents' attention (even if they scold them and drag them back to bed).

What if they feel that they can't sleep if left alone? You can try different approaches. One is actually being in their bedroom until they fall asleep, but without intervening. You just sit there and stare at the wall (or you put on your headphones and listen to your favorite podcast). Tell them it's time to go to bed. No more singing, no more reprimands either. Just shush them and tell them it's time to sleep. If possible, don't even make eye contact. The purpose is to provide some comfort while keeping this moment as boring as possible! Another possibility is to use some sleep training method that slowly removes this "sleep crotch," something like the disappearing chair approach (Rowell, 2014).

Once your toddler is old enough to understand they have to stay in bed, you can reward them by coming back every couple of minutes and giving them a soft kiss on their forehead if they don't call you. You do so until you find they are asleep. And the next morning, you prize them with a little shiny sticker for their window pane or a smiley face of syrup on their pancakes!

Aggression Towards Other Children

Sometimes a toddler can become aggressive, especially towards other siblings or children they meet in daycare, or while playing in the park. It can be awkward when your toddler pushes, yells, takes a toy from another child's hands, or even bites! The first thing you should understand is that toddlers are still self-centered like babies. While you can teach them the first social skills, such as taking turns, you can't expect the same for sharing: Hey, even we adults don't like sharing! How do you feel when your partner takes all the covers in bed, or if someone you have just met asks you to take a look at your new smartphone?

Besides, toddlers like playing *near* other children, but they still don't play *with* other children: Toddlers "engage in parallel play; they will play next to each other, but they won't really interact. Interactive play comes when toddlers are a little older or reach the preschool years" (Phillips, 2014). Sharing happens when children play together and the toys are part of the game. How can you prevent a tantrum or aggression because of toys? You can distract them with another toy, you can remove them from the scene (for example, if they start to cry about a toy that belongs to another child), or you can anticipate they'll have trouble sharing and suggest choosing specific toys they are not particularly attached to for bringing to the playground. In any case, if they throw a tantrum about sharing you should understand it is a normal stage.

Pushing, hitting, or biting, usually appear when children lack the means to express their emotions otherwise. Of course, you can't let them get away with this kind of behavior. Never hit them back or bite them back! Remember that they learn from observing you. On the contrary, remove your toddler from the place, and explain to them they can play once they learn it's not okay to bite or push. Make sure the bitten child is okay, show your concern, and after your toddler has calmed down, help them make amends for their behavior. But don't scold them or lecture them for too long. If they learn they get your attention through these undesired behaviors, they will do them over and over again. Instead, teach them "other ways to deal with frustration (perhaps by saying, "Help!" or "I'm mad!"), showing extra concern for the child who was bitten, and offering biters a snack to chomp on instead" (Phillips, 2014). If the behavior repeats, you should talk to your pediatrician and express your concern.Being Rude and Disrespectful to Parents

Toddlers still don't have those verbal abilities that will exasperate you once they reach their teenage years! And still, they can be rude sometimes. Correct them if they use a loud tone of voice, or if they don't say 'please' and "thank you" but, what's more important, set an example and treat them as you expect to be treated. If you are losing your temper and you scream at your toddler, they will scream louder.

More serious situations, such as swearing at the parent, or name-calling, don't apply to the majority of toddlers but may arise later with preschoolers. If a toddler copies their siblings, the first thing you have to do is address this negative behavior in your older children. Again, begin by asking yourself where are they getting this from. If you call them names, they will call them back at you, or others. Or is it possible someone is being aggressive to them at school?

Try talking to your older children, not in the middle of an argument but during a calm time. Explain to them how these verbal aggressions make you feel, and ask them how they would feel if someone did that to them. Showing empathy is the best way to teach it. If your toddler is copying the behavior of their brothers and sisters, you can also ask for your older child's help: "[Toddler's name] is learning from you, and they look up to you. They could get in trouble if they learn it's okay to swear or to call names. I need your help teaching them good manners. I'm sure you can do it!"

If the toddler pushes the parent, hits you, or spits at you, this should be treated the same as when they direct their aggression toward other children. These behaviors tell that they are angry, sad, or frustrated, and can't let it out otherwise. While you teach them another way of expressing these feelings (which are unpleasant, but normal and valid), don't get mad at them. Show them that you are sad and that you don't want to play with them if they become aggressive. That's also teaching them the natural consequence of their actions. But at the same time, make sure you still show your toddler your unconditional love. Unlike their classmates, you won't stop loving them no matter how poorly they behave. Of course, one thing is to love them and another thing is to accept these aggressions and not make a big deal out of them.

Something that can really drive parents mad is when the toddler starts using the word 'no' for everything. Sometimes, the use of *no* comes out of their need to display independence: Put on some socks. No! Brush your teeth. No! Here, have some more juice. No! Even when they actually want to say yes! You ask them if they want another slice of apple, and they say *no*, and the next thing you know, they are crying when you eat the last bite. In fact, they may be lacking the vocabulary for saying *yes*!

A good strategy for avoiding constant defiance is offering the toddler choices, even when they are a request in disguise. Instead of telling them to go brush their teeth, you can say "Would you rather brush your teeth now, or after putting on your pajamas?" This leaves the toddler in the belief they have some control. Also, it allows you to replace your own NOs. If you often use this word, your toddler—you've guessed it!—will copy you! Instead of "No, you can't have a bar of chocolate for dessert," you can try "You can have a banana, a string of cheese, or three strawberries for dessert. Which one do you want?"

Another behavior of toddlers that parents can find rude is their tendency to constantly interrupt you while you speak. Correct them, of course, always gently. But also, pay attention: Is it possible that you too are interrupting them whenever they try to tell you something? Your toddler may be telling you for the fourth time in a row how they found a snail among their gardening tools. For you, it's already old information so you take a look at your phone while they are speaking. For them, it's still the most important thing in the world. Be kind to them, empathize, and practice active listening whenever you have the chance.

Does Time Out Work?

It is one of the most popular discipline methods among parents. But does it work with a toddler? The problem with the time-out is that it was not created as a punishment but as a distraction from an over-stimulating environment that is causing the child to misbehave. Instead of isolating and restricting the child's movement, and later lecturing them, the whole purpose of time-out is to place the child "into a non-reinforcing place to calm down and feel safe" (Li, 2022).

Once you tell a toddler to go to their room for a time-out, don't expect them to "reflect" on their poor behavior, which they won't. A minute after you've sent them, they'll get distracted by something else, and once you arrive to try and reason with them, most likely they will have forgotten already about what caused the time-out in the first place!

For toddlers, it's better to switch the classic "time-out" for a "time-in." Stay with them during the time-out, again, not lecturing but distracting them from whatever caused the bad behavior in the first place. Don't reward the negative behavior, but always address their emotions! Being acknowledged is sometimes everything the toddler needs to start calming down and self-soothing: "You are feeling angry because you wanted pizza instead of spinach."

As in any temper tantrum, you need to understand misbehaving as a lack of control, the toddler being overwhelmed by their emotions, so this is not the time for a lecture on food waste whatsoever. Only after the toddler has calmed down, should you address the behavior that caused the need for the time-in: *I know you threw away the spinach because you don't like it. We don't waste food. You can leave it on your plate instead.* Unlike the time-out, which leaves them alone and further increases their frustration, the time-in is a moment of reflection and learning: "You can talk to them about their feelings and motivations for their behavior, giving them time to think aloud and come up with solutions for how to handle conflict when they come back to play" (Davies, 2020).

So, going back to the situation at the greengrocer's we talked about at the beginning of the chapter, if you apply positive parenting there are some ways you can approach it:

- Because you know your toddler, you are aware he's tired from being at the park. It's great that you picked him up, but you should also anticipate that you are going to put him down: "We need to buy carrots and bananas for dinner. You like them, don't you? So I'm going to put you down now. Soon, we'll get home."

- If the toddler picks a tomato, the right thing to do is to ask for it back or to tell them to return it to its place because it's not theirs. You can create in them a sense of control if you give them a choice: "Would you like to hand me the tomato? Or do you want to put it back in the box?" Taking the tomato from their hand creates frustration, which mixed up with tiredness (and possibly, hunger) creates a meltdown.

- If your toddler puts back the tomato, you praise him for his good behavior. You pay for your groceries and you can give him a banana to eat along the way since your hands are full and you can no longer carry him up. This little reward may be all that he needs to walk calmly to your door!

- And if the temper tantrum still happens... You know there is no way you can reason with him at the time. You won't be able to go on shopping, and you know scolding him only makes things worse. In this case, keeping realistic expectations means taking him out of the scenery, going back home, and setting for frozen beans this time. You can talk to him once he is calmer, and state that next time, if he behaves better at the greengrocer's, you can cook carrots instead. Who would have guessed? The answer was A!

Chapter Takeaways

- Toddlers misbehave when they don't know how to behave otherwise, or when they are overpassed by emotions, or if they are trying to call your attention. Positive parenting focuses on the cause of the behavior and acts in consequence. Even more, we try to anticipate certain situations to prevent misbehaving altogether.

- Temper tantrums are normal in toddlers, but they become a problem when preschoolers or even older children are not given the tools to handle them. They usually occur when the toddler is lacking the words to express their emotion, and even the ability to recognize it. You can help them by anticipating what's going to happen, validating their feelings by putting them into words, or distracting them.

- During the rage of the temper tantrum, there is no possible negotiation. Just keep your toddler from harming themselves or others and wait for the meltdown to fade. Address the behavior later without punishment.

- Mealtimes are sometimes problematic situations, either because the toddler gets impatient or because they are picky eaters. While giving them choices and involving them in the preparation of meals can help, you should never force a toddler to eat. If they get hungry, teach them it is the natural consequence of their decision, and refrain from giving them snacks.

- Bedtime tantrums can be usually prevented through a consistent, predictable routine. Avoiding screen time, carefully choosing the best bedtime according to your toddler's inner clock, and being empathic with their nighttime fears, together with some gentle sleep training methods, all of this can help them stay in bed and sleep better at night.

- While toddlers still don't engage in cooperative play, they can still learn some basic social behavior. Try to set them with clear rules and guide them through examples. If they have trouble sharing, prevent aggressions by taking them away from problematic situations.

- If your toddler drives you crazy saying no to everything, try offering them choices to give them a sense of being in control.

- Time-outs should be replaced by time-ins: Don't leave your toddler alone when you take them away from a situation. Instead, use this time to stay with them, refrain them from hurting themselves or any other person, and address their feelings. Only after they have calmed down, can you talk about the negative behavior and how to fix it.

Positive parenting is about raising confident, happy children. The better they understand their limits, the more they'll respect them, and the better they'll behave. In the following chapter, we will take a further look at ways we can encourage good behavior instead of only correcting bad ones.

Chapter 4

Praise Is Better Than Prize!

The best way to make children good is to make them happy. −Oscar Wilde

Research studies show that positive parenting has a long-lasting effect on children and teenagers. These kids behave better, have better grades at school, engage in positive social interactions, and have better mental health, such as higher self-esteem, lower risk of depression and anxiety, and higher expectations towards their future (Smokowski et alt., 2014).

So as challenging as it may be to unlearn the old parenting ways and give up reactive parenting towards proactive parenting, think about positive parenting as a long-time investment. Sure, it may be easier now to just let your toddler get away with it. It may be easier to simply punish them or scorn them if they are noisy during your Zoom meeting. But as they grow, it will get harder.

On the other hand, now that you have a toddler it may take a lot of effort on your part to breathe down, count to 10, and connect before correcting. But positive parenting will pay off. It will become easier in time. Trust me: I have a girl in elementary school who I don't need to bribe or yell at for her to help around the house. She is happy to set the table and even picks up the glasses for her younger brothers matching the boys' favorite colors. It's not magic: Positive parenting works!

How can we promote good behavior in our children from an early age? Isn't rewarding similar to bribing? Does any child really *want* to behave as expected? Or are we manipulating them somehow? After reading this chapter, we will have solved these and other doubts that may have come up.

Don't Reinforce Negative Behavior

We have already seen that most of the toddler's negative behavior is a call for attention. So every time you react, you are actually providing them with all that attention they long for! If you are working on keeping your cool and remaining calm, that's great! If you manage to avoid reacting at least on most occasions, you are already interrupting the cycle of reinforcement.

However, you have to be careful, because there is yet another way many parents accidentally reinforce misbehaving: Giving in! (Morin, 2022):

If a parent tells a child they can't go outside, but then the child begs and pleads until the parent gives in, the child's whining has been positively reinforced. The child learned that whining helps them get what they want, encouraging them to whine again in the future.

Once you have set a limit, stick to it. The same applies when your partner or spouse sets the limit: You may disagree on it, but in front of your toddler you have to work as a team. If one of you says something is forbidden and the other one allows it, it will create confusion for the child at first, but then, they'll learn to take advantage. This can also cause marital problems (more on this later on).

What if you make a mistake? For example, if you decided on a strict "no staying up after 8 p.m." policy, and your partner makes you realize you are being too strict. If you didn't believe your toddler when they claimed their tummy hurt because you thought they were trying to skip the broccoli, only to see them throw up shortly after? Or if you lose your cool after all, and you end up saying something hurtful to your child (such as what I did sometimes when my daughter spilled her cup)?

Kelly Holmes, the author of the book *Happy You, Happy Family*, suggests applying the "Magic 5:1 Ratio." After forgiving yourself (you are only human) and apologizing to your toddler, "after you've lost it with your child, make sure to get five positive interactions on the books as fast as possible" (Holmes, 2016). If you said something horrible, try to commit to at least five positive acts during that day, which can include hugs, kisses, a loving phrase, smiling at them while looking straight into their eyes, singing them a song, or whatever other little act that makes both of your hearts get close once again.

Showing through the example to recognize you have made a mistake, apologizing, and making amends, is also a great way to guide your child through imitation! In time, they'll learn to recognize their wrongdoings and try to make things right.

Now, let's go to positive behavior! What shall you do when your toddler is doing something right? Instead of simply taking it for granted, or considering yourself lucky for at least having a break, you can invest in acknowledging and rewarding good acts. This way, they'll become more frequent!

Rewarding Positive Behavior

Remember how I mentioned before that positive parenting considers children inherently good? This implies that you should always try to put your focus on the things that your toddler achieves, on the occasions they are up to the task, on the times they answer appropriately or display good manners. In other words, you should put your focus on their good behaviors, and not on the problematic ones. And putting your focus means giving them more attention. How can you show your child that you are noticing the good they do? Easy: You reward good behavior!

But before getting into specific tips you can implement starting today, let's define "reward." Not every author agrees on what should or shouldn't be considered an appropriate reward for a child. While Amy Morin from *Very Well Family* accepts the eventual little presents, such as stickers or even money (Morin, 2022), experts such as Amy McCready refute the idea of "reward" and state we should change it for "encouragement" (McCready, 2021):

Kids who are rewarded often are likely to lose interest in the activity they're being rewarded for, whether it's music practice or playing nicely with a sibling. They become more interested in the rewards, meaning you may have to keep up the rewards to maintain the same quality of behavior.

In any case, rewards don't need to be material. Rewards can be kind words, or displays of affection such as pats on the back, a high-five, or a thumbs-up. And the best reward you can give to your toddler is your positive attention: As they notice some behavior is making you notice, they are likely to repeat it in the future! So no, by rewarding we don't mean you should "bribe" your child by paying them for doing household chores or for getting good grades at school! In fact, parents who decide to give them money for what would otherwise be considered expected behavior, tend to find out that children focus more on the reward itself, and begin to ask for more to achieve the same results.

Encouragement, on the other side, is the best way to create long-lasting self-confidence and build healthy self-esteem. This way, children learn that to make the right choices, and the good feeling they get from being recognized and praised is all the reward they need to keep going! However, parents should put a lot of attention on *when* providing praise: If you only say nice things to a child when they get the desired result, they could get easily frustrated when things don't come out as expected and give up. Therefore, instead of praising your toddler for making their bed (something that is likely to require your supervision and assistance), praise them *as soon as they start attempting* the chore, no matter if the results turn out less than perfect: "It's so kind of you to help me make your bed!"

The same works for older children: Don't praise your kid when they get an A in their math exam, because this way you are rewarding the result. Praise them during the process! "I see you are committed and concentrated on studying for your test. That's great!" Part of being a positive parent is showing them your unconditional love, so you don't want to instill in your children the idea that you love them when they are good. They won't always get A's in their exams, but if they don't do so well, they will still know you value them for trying.

You shouldn't praise them for their looks. You will always find your children beautiful, but they will go through awkward stages, and once they look into the mirror and they can barely recognize themselves behind all that acne, they may find it hard to buy when you claim they "are as pretty as ever." Besides, you don't want them to build their self-esteem on the outside, right? Similarly, you don't want to praise them for something they are naturally good at, such as their personality: "You are such a great friend!" That's labeling, even if it looks nice. Instead, praise them for specific actions they take and you want to reinforce: "It was so kind of you to lend your bucket to Sarah in the playground. Look how happy she is!"

Teaching Them About Choices and Consequences

Positive reinforcement helps the children build confidence in themselves. By showing them you trust them to make their decisions, but still guiding them by explaining to them the consequences, your children will learn from their mistakes and there will be no need to punish them. Let's say your child doesn't want to wear a swimsuit for going to the beach, and she wants to wear a pink skirt, you can tell them: "If you don't wear a swimsuit, you won't be able to play with water or else your favorite skirt will get wet." Later, when they *do* want to play at the seaside, you can remind them they had the choice to put on a swimsuit. They will listen to you next time!

According to Amy Morin, "enforcing natural consequences can turn poor choices into learning opportunities" (Morin, 2022), as long as your child is capable of such behavior (here is important once again to keep realistic expectations), the consequence is fair and respectful (they may opt out of a swimsuit, but don't let them *choose* to wear sunscreen, just put it on them, please!), and you let them know in advance the probable outcome of their choice (this way, because you told them they wouldn't get to play with water, it doesn't feel like a punishment).

But teaching about natural consequences can also reinforce *good* behavior, and thus, lead them to repeat the right choices. You can offer your toddler some kind of reward that is directly connected to what they did, to the decisions they took. "This connection between the reinforcement and the behavior will make the positive consequence more memorable and effective" (Morin, 2022). Here are some examples:

- "You are being so kind, helping me in the garden and raking all those leaves. I'm thinking we should put this brand new flower pot wherever you like!"

- "Because you are setting the table for dinner, I have some free time on my hands. How about I start preparing your lunchbox, so later we have more time for another bedtime story?"

- "I really admire what a good sport you were when your brother beat you at that game. Would you like to play again with me?"

- "You are sitting so still while I trim your nails!

Good for you! Would you like to listen to your favorite song while I finish with your other hand?"

As we have seen, if you are going to reward your toddler, it's better if it's through something intangible, such as giving them a choice for something they like or spending more time with them. Nothing means more to our toddlers than the moments we share with them providing undivided attention!

Creating Positive Routines

If you live with a toddler, then you've probably found out that the only way to make it through the day is by keeping lots of routines: You have a morning routine, a daycare routine (or a routine for staying at home), you have fixed times for meals, you probably do your shopping some specific days of the week. Then, of course, it is the bathtime routine, the naptime routine, and the dreaded yet much-needed bedtime routine. You have routines for taking public transport or for long car drives. You have routines when having doctor's appointments. You even have to set up some sort of routine when you are on holiday.

What exactly is a routine? Stephen Altrogge defines it as "a sequence of actions that you do repeatedly," such as waking up at a specific time, having a cup of coffee for breakfast, brushing your teeth before dressing up, etc. "They're all actions that happen again and again, a rhythm in your daily life" (Altrogge, 2019). Not every routine is necessary, or even good for you. Because they are made from habits, you don't have to think them through, you just do them. You are used to things being a certain way and, as we have seen in previous chapters, it's hard to unlearn.

When you have a baby, you include them into your routine, or you make adjustments to your old routine to deal with the fact that now you are a parent, and there is a little person you need to look after. By the time they are toddlers, children are used to their lives being structured in routines. However, if your toddler dislikes specific parts of their routine, chances are that complaining, whining, crying, nagging, or even throwing tantrums will also become a part of their routine. And that's exactly what makes it too hard for us to enjoy parenting! It's one thing if our kid is having a bad day. But what if most days are bad? Nobody can get used to having a long row of bad days turning into their normal life. Believe me: It doesn't have to be this way. Your daily or weekly routine *can* be enjoyable!

You can't just keep making changes trying to prevent mealtime tantrums or evening fussiness. Toddlers need anticipation! Unexpected changes can turn them insecure and have repercussions on their mood and sleep quality. Besides, because you have so many things to take care of, the more structured your routine, the easier your life gets. Plus, having routines makes special occasions, well, *more* special! The key is creating positive routines.

Try to take some notes (whether in an actual notebook or your mind) of what a typical day of your toddler's life looks like. Which are the moments that usually create more tension? Are there specific parts of your day in which you struggle to keep your cool and the child seems to get more difficult than usual? Perhaps, the answer is making a small adjustment to that routine.

- Is it hard to wake them up in the morning? Do they look tired and moody? They are probably not getting enough sleep at night. Try switching their bedtime to an earlier time, or establishing sleep hygiene so they can rest properly and wake up feeling refreshed.

- Are you always complaining they take forever to finish their breakfast? Maybe they are not hungry, and you could replace the tower of pancakes with light fresh-squeezed orange juice and a banana. Or maybe, you can set the alarm clock 15 minutes earlier, and let your toddler have breakfast at their pace without worrying it will get late.

- Is dressing them up a struggle because they want to put on the clothes by themselves? Or maybe they refuse to wear matching shoes no matter what. In any case, laying down the clothes the night before, together with your toddler so they at least have a saying, may ease things up.

- Does it take forever to leave home—even if it's for something your toddler enjoys, such as visiting their cousins, or going out for an ice cream—because they take such a long time putting on their shoes and their jacket? Anticipation is the key here! No toddler wants to delay immediate pleasure (for example, putting away the blocks they are playing with) for a later reward (such as playing with their cousins). However, if you talk to them an hour before leaving and you start preparing in advance, they may be ready before you.

Some positive changes you can start implementing to your routine that are likely to improve your life, as well as your toddler's, include

- rising early
- having a proper breakfast

- eating healthy

- doing some exercise (later on, we'll explain the benefits of outdoor play for toddlers)

- listening to music

- reciting affirmations, or making positive statements (such as praising your toddler)

- being grateful for what you've already got (you are healthy, you have a healthy child, you have a home, food on your plate, etc.)

- no screen time an hour before bedtime (toddlers and adults alike)

- making plans for the next day

- acknowledging at least three achievements before going to sleep

Of course, no matter how much you love your life, some parts of everyone's routine are less than enjoyable. You may love having pets at home, but cleaning your cat's litter box is surely no picnic! The same happens to your toddler: They may complain about having to make the bed, carry their backpack all the way to the daycare center, or brush their teeth. Praise can help you, but you can also explain to them that when the part of their routine they don't like is complete, then there is time for the things they enjoy the most (McCready, 2021). For example, they have more time to play outside after having lunch if they first brush their teeth.

Outdoor Play and Exploring

Because it helps them develop physically, mentally, as well as emotionally, teaching them to be independent and confident, positive parenting embraces outdoor play from the time babies are born to well into their teenage years.

In every toddler's routine, there should be plenty of time for outdoor playing. Sometimes this is difficult to achieve because we live in crowded cities, in small apartments, and find ourselves pretty busy during the week. We shouldn't blame ourselves if we can't bring our toddler to the playground every single day, but we should do our best to make it our goal. Of course, if we have a backyard, a terrace, or a patio, it gets easier! If possible, it's better to have toddlers and preschoolers spending their free time outside several times a day.

But why is it such a big deal? If they have plenty of toys inside, do they still need to go out so often? After all, when they go out, toddlers get dirty! They make a mess, they try to do dangerous things such as tree-climbing, and they can even get insect bites. I know, it takes some effort from your side because toddlers need constant supervision. And yet, the benefits they get from outdoor activities surpass the cons. Taking some basic precautions, such as always applying sunscreen and insect repellent, making sure there are no hazardous elements at their reach—rakes, spades, the lawn mower, herbicide, etc.—spending time outside with your toddler is a great way of connecting with them.

By playing outdoors, your toddler gains motor skills and exercises in a natural way (they don't need to practice a sport or even play ruled games at this age, exercising comes from their natural movements and impulses to explore their surroundings). Let your toddler run, hide, jump, kick a ball, or chase a butterfly! Their world gets bigger when they have access to big outdoor areas. As you let them engage in free play, they gain confidence in their abilities and become more independent. Still, remember that by this time they have no sense of danger, so you have to keep an eye on them all the time, even if you are in a private space.

More time outdoors means less screen time! This helps them better develop their sight. According to *Raising Children*, a respected Australian parenting site, "Spending time outdoors might lower your child's chances of developing short-sightedness. Also, some safe play in the sun can be good too—small amounts of sunlight exposure can help boost vitamin D levels" (Raising Children Network, 2019). Apart from providing benefits for their physical well-being, outdoor play calms children down, relaxes them, and it improves their sleep quality. Nothing like spending a long morning playing in the backyard for taking a nice, long nap after lunch!

Of course, when children play outside, their hands, face, and clothes get dirty. Let them wear comfortable clothes and don't worry about dirt stains! Teach them to wash their hands and encourage healthy habits when spending time outdoors, such as drinking more water.

Playing outside is also a great booster for your child's imagination. When they are among the plants and the trees, and running along with their family's pet, your child is daydreaming, creating new fantasy worlds in which they get to live all sorts of adventures. Free outdoor playing is linked with longer attention spans, which makes it perfect for impatient, fussy toddlers.

Besides, your child gets to spend some time connecting with nature, learning from their direct experiences—what they see, hear, touch, smell, and even taste if you have some veggies growing!—and spending all that toddler energy they accumulate and would otherwise become misbehaving (don't worry, I'll give you some tips for indoor activities for those long, rainy days!). As they grow close to plants, insects, and other animals, toddlers learn easily to love and respect them. A simple tip is to encourage them through positive statements:

- Instead of "Don't pick the flowers," opt for, "We can pick the flowers that are already on the grass."

- Instead of "Don't touch the butterfly, you can hurt it!" try, "It's beautiful to look at the butterfly and let it fly freely, right?"

- Or avoid "Don't step on the grass," and change it to "We walk on the paths."

By the way, notice how positive statements *describe* a situation instead of giving an order. This way, your toddler learns the rule without being constrained.

Ideas For Outdoor Play

- Include some elements that your toddler can play with that are age-appropriate: A ball, a bucket, a toy gardening set, or a skipping rope (no, they won't skip yet, but they can drag it around, tie it to a tree, or pretend it's something else).

PRAISE IS BETTER THAN PRIZE! 101

- You can also let them use a tricycle or a scooter, but get them used to helmets, and knee and elbow pads the whole time.

- Try to engage with your toddler during some moments of their play, and allow them free play for other times. Once they become preschoolers, they'll love playing tag or hide-and-seek! In the meantime, when playing with a young toddler, allow them to guide you in their activities, don't overwhelm them with ruled games.

- Your toddler can help you with gardening activities, such as removing weeds, planting seeds, or watering the plants, as long as you supervise them and show them how!

- If your toddler gets over excited when going out, allow them to run freely for a while, and later attract their attention to something that keeps them calm and observant: An ant carrying a huge leaf, the little drops of morning dew on the plants, the birds building a nest, or the sounds of a nearby insect. Toddlers are curious by nature! Seize this opportunity to teach them something new.

- Make sure they wear the appropriate clothes for each season: In the summer, you can let them splash and play with water. In winter, they can still go out as long as they are wearing warm clothes.

- Think about some activities your child can't do at home and let them try them outside, such as playing with sand (or dirt!), blowing bubbles, finger painting, or splashing water by carrying it around in plastic Tupperware! It's also better to help them climb a tree than to scold them for climbing on their older brother's bunk bed. When given the chance to try new things and explore their capacities, and once they realize they can do all of those when playing outdoors, chances are they won't try them inside again.

Managing And Controlling Digital Use

The American Academy of Pediatrics and the American Psychological Association strongly recommend that children should have no screen exposure at all until they are 18 months old, except for video calls. Toddlers from 18 to 24 months should only get limited screen time, only high-quality programming, and watch it together with their parents. Children aged two to five should have only one hour of screen exposure (APA, 2019).

However, technology is a part of our world, whether we like it or not. Teaching your children about it will help them achieve healthier interactions. Technology should be considered as a challenge, but not as a danger. "Explain that tablets, computers and other media devices are not toys, and should be handled with care. Discuss with kids the many benefits of technology as well as the risks" (APA, 2019). These conversations should become more fluid and frequent the older the child gets. A toddler will not have access to the Internet the same way a scholar does. You have to set the right example: If you can't refrain from staring at your phone or if the TV is always on, there's no way your children will accept the boundaries. If possible, refrain from purchasing their own devices. Toddlers don't "need" tablets to have fun!

Spending one-on-one time together and taking your toddler to play outside several times a day goes hand in hand with reducing screen time! Set clear limits, such as timers, or allow your toddler to watch "one more episode" of their favorite cartoon instead of "15 more minutes," which can lead to frustration and throwing tantrums.

At the same time, remember that flexibility is important for setting those limits. If your toddler needs a little more screen time because you are traveling abroad and the plane got delayed, it won't harm them or turn you into a neglectful parent! In the same way, if they spent half an hour in a video chat with their grandparents, don't take this from their allowed playtime with their educational app.

In any case, you can't forbid your toddler from spending some time in front of the screen. You can—and should—limit that time and make sure they only access high-quality content appropriate for their age.

More Engaging Activities

As you can see, when your toddler is busy and they find motivation in fun, engaging activities, chances are they'll behave better. Again, it is crucial that you accept your child's current capacities and don't label certain actions that are normal for their age as "misbehaving." For instance, throwing all the blocks from a box into the floor before playing with them is less than ideal if someone is walking barefoot and happens to step on one, but for your child, it's part of the exploration.

I already gave you some ideas for playing outside. Here are more engaging activities that can keep your toddler busy and happy!

Art and Crafts

From coloring books to painting on the floor with a paintbrush and some water, from creating a scrapbook (cutting papers with their fingers only) to making a macaroni necklace, children enjoy themselves a lot when they are expressing their creativity through different materials. The result is the least important! What matters the most is that they have fun.

Books

You don't need your baby to utter their first words to talk to them: You probably started talking to your toddler from the day they were born, right? In the same way, despite your toddler being too young for recognizing letters or words, they can still "read" or play with books! If you have some time on your hands, sharing a story is a wonderful way to connect, expand their vocabulary, and keep them quiet and calm for a while. But as soon as toddlers are left alone with their books, they'll amuse themselves by passing on the pages, looking at the pictures, and sometimes, even reading aloud the story you have told them over and over.

Music

Listening to their favorite song, singing along, or dancing, all of these are great activities for your toddler. You can create playlists appropriate for different moments of the day: Fun music for playing indoors, dancing with scarves, or doing a little choreography, and calm, soft music for the hour before their bedtime routine. Toddlers also enjoy playing music, and the best part is you don't need an instrument: Banging two spoons on the table, shaking homemade maracas, or blowing into a bottle are great examples of how to make music with the things you have at home.

Dressing Up

Another great activity for a rainy day is emptying a drawer of your clothes and allowing your toddler to dress up. They can try on anything they like! A shirt, a hat, some of your necklaces… Dressing up is a great way of improving their fine motor, without the pressure to hurry up buttoning that shirt because it's time to go. Sometimes, you can include role-playing in the game! Let your toddler pretend to be "mummy" or "daddy" and have fun impersonating them!

Household Chores

You may be really busy at home, and think that there is no way you can entertain your toddler at the same time. But did you know they could help you in many ways? You can give them a clean rag and let them dust the bookcase, you can teach them how to sweep with their toy broom, or feed their pet.

Besides learning useful skills, they will boost their self-esteem if you let them know how much you appreciate their help.

Transferring Activities

Pouring liquids from one vase to another; scooping buttons, crackers, cereals, or grapes; or transferring materials such as kinetic sand, rice, or shaving foam from one recipient to another are great ways to keep a toddler quiet and focused. With these games, they learn basic math concepts, such as quantity, cause and effect, or weight, while they practice their fine motor (Punkoney, 2012).

Sorting

The same as transferring, sorting objects allows your toddler to naturally acquire some basic math skills. Identifying the common traits among a group of objects is great for developing their attention and logical thought. Buttons, coins, legumes, seeds, cereals, keys… You can give them any kind of object to sort, as long as they have already stopped putting small things into their mouth. If your toddler enjoys sorting activities, then you can turn tidying up time into a game! Putting away their toys in the right box, or finding matching socks, could be fun!

An Indoor Playground

If a rainy day is keeping your toddler bouncing against the walls, you can create an indoor obstacle course by simply moving some furniture. You can also set a tent with blankets, and let them jump, not on their beds, but on a mattress on the floor; you can create a fort with boxes, or turn them into a cardboard train with some paint and glue. Sure, later you have to tidy up, but your toddler will have a great time and stop complaining about how they can't go out.

Chapter Takeaways

- While becoming a positive parent may seem challenging at first, it pays in the long run, as children will naturally tend to behave better with our guidance.

- Giving in or scolding your child when they misbehave still provides them with attention, so we should avoid that if we don't want to reinforce certain negative behaviors.

- Positive parenting puts most of the focus on the good behavior of a toddler and tries to reinforce it through rewards (mostly immaterial) and praise.

- Encouraging your child for their good behavior—not for their results or their natural traits—leads them to repeat such behavior, as they find inner reward more fulfilling than a material prize.

- Positive parenting also teaches children the natural consequences of their decisions, so that in the future they learn to make the right choices. It's not a punishment or a bribe if the consequence directly depends on what the child did or did not do!

- Spending plenty of time outdoors has a lot of benefits for your child's physical, emotional, and social well-being. While outdoor play allows them to spend all that extra toddler energy, it also helps them calm down and behave better in other moments of the day.

- Every expert recommends that toddlers spend little time in front of the screens. While you should control and limit their access to technology, you should not be too rigid or consider it a threat. Setting clear limits while being flexible on special occasions is likely to help your toddler acquire better self-control when using devices.

- If your toddler is happily playing something engaging, they are likely to behave better, even on long, rainy afternoons!

We have seen many strategies positive parenting implements for reinforcing good behavior in toddlers. It's great to let your child know how much you love them! And even better it is teaching them to love themselves, so the following chapter will focus on confidence building.

Chapter 5

Paving The Way to Self-Esteem

Teach them well and let them lead the way / Show them all the beauty they possess inside / Give them a sense of pride to make it easier. –Whitney Houston

On those long days when your toddler is full of energy and you run out of it; when your head is exploding from taking mental notes of everything you have to do before allowing yourself to finally get in bed, and your toddler refuses to take a much-needed nap; when you are feeling under the weather but your toddler comes up with a fever and you have to reach for the car keys and drive them to the ER... you may forget that their childhood is just a phase and that it will soon pass. However, your job as a parent has just begun.

Achieving your toddler to stay still while waiting for the bus, or being quiet in the supermarket line is possible through many parenting approaches: An authoritarian parent will handle it by eliciting fear of getting in trouble; a permissive parent may just give in and buy them all sorts of snacks; a positive parent will help the child understand the situation, accept their emotions as they appear, and learn from the natural consequences of their actions.

In a not-so-distant future, your toddler will be a teenager in high school, and the goal will change from refraining from throwing a temper tantrum to getting good grades in their exams. An authoritarian parent may impose on their children a strict study routine, taking away their phones, and forbidding them to go out for several weekends. A permissive parent may try to offer all sorts of rewards and compensations if their kids do well, hoping that receiving a new laptop, a trip abroad, or their first car will get them studying, but these won't necessarily work (they could end up cheating, for example!). A positive parent will anticipate the tension the exams generate in teens, help them deal with these emotions, and trust their decisions when it comes to being responsible. By now, these parents have provided their children with valuable tools and they know what to expect from them without pushing them beyond their capacities.

While the three kids may end up passing the exams eventually, only the positive parenting style will turn up with a happy, confident teen that will sit through their tests fully committed, and confident they'll do their best. And even if the results turn out worse than expected, their self-esteem will allow them to recover from that experience and learn from their mistakes. They know that their parents' love does not depend on a grade, but they still know the better they do in school, the further they'll get in their careers.

Being a positive parent means accepting that your job is not to get a child that sits still and gets good grades, but rather a confident child that understands and manages their emotions, that is open to communicating, and that trusts you no matter what. And you, as a parent, should start building that confidence and boosting their self-esteem from a very young age.

How can you help your toddler deal with unpleasant feelings, such as discomfort or frustration without giving in or scolding them? What are the best ways of teaching them values that will last for their whole lifetimes, such as empathy, responsibility, and accountability? It's a delicate balance, but we can give you some valuable tips in this chapter.

Confidence Building

Confident children are happier, get better results in school, interact better with their parents and their peers, are not afraid of attempting new things and can recover faster from failure. Helping your child build healthy self-esteem is part of your job as a parent. How do you do it?

Express Your Love Every Day in Many Ways

Children feel good about themselves when they know they are loved. Saying positive affirmations to your child should not be limited to praising their good behavior. Tell them that you love them, that you are proud of them, or that they are an amazing person, without being a specific reason for it! A spontaneous hug, a pat on the head, looking into their eyes, and smiling... All of these little gestures go a long way to making a child feel special and loved.

What's most important is spending quality time connecting with your toddler: I insist, 10 minutes a day is enough for making a difference. Listening to them, watching them play, and letting them know that you are seeing them, even if they didn't show you: "I see you are climbing on the big slide, I'm proud of you!"

Avoid Empty Praise

Most of us are used to answering "that's nice," "great job," "good for you," or "awesome" whenever our child shares something with us. The problem with these lines is that more often than not, they come in automatic mode, and don't do anything for your child (The Pragmatic Parent, 2016):

Saying "good job" becomes a habit when we're not fully engaged with our kids and looking for a quick handout that will pacify them. Not only will kids learn to expect praise if you give it to them every time they have an accomplishment or want to show you something, but they will also learn that your praise is insincere.

To show your child that you are really putting attention to them, you have to praise specific parts of their behavior or results: "You put a lot of detail into this picture, look at how big are the elephant's ears!" or "You are being really careful while playing with your baby sister, that's very kind of you." These statements show your child not only that you care, but that you are noticing them for real. This is a true self-esteem boost!

Set the Example

How can we expect our children to persevere and learn from their mistakes if we are constantly scolding ourselves or giving up when things don't go as planned? Always keep in mind your child is copying you! So for example, if I had a bad day at work because I planned a lesson that didn't go well, I should avoid using statements such as "I'm not good at teaching!" or "That's it, I blew it." Instead, I try to say things such as "Today was not a good day, I'll try to do better tomorrow." Learning to deal with your own frustrations and accepting that things can go wrong sometimes is a valuable lesson for you, but for your children as well.

Embrace Their Natural Good Skills

Some toddlers learn to climb a ladder or to jump on one foot before they can utter two-word sentences, the same as some children are better at math and others are great at sports. While some parents are worried that their kid may be "left behind" in certain areas, and push them into the activities they don't do so well, positive parenting will do otherwise: Let your child spend more time doing something they are already good at! Of course, if your child needs speech therapy you will still have them do all the exercises, but don't reduce their outdoor playtime if they are great at climbing. In the same way, if your child is great with music but not so good at sports, sign them up in a school band instead of forcing them to take part in the soccer team.

This is because your goal is not to raise a child that excels in every single area, but a confident child: "While self-confidence tends to be situational, it is also transferrable. That is, often when you feel brave in one area of their life then these feelings tend to merge into other areas" (Grose, 2017). Dr. William Sears, the main authority for the attachment parenting style, also recommends having a Wall of Fame at home for showing your children how much you value their individual accomplishments: "Every child is good at something. Discover it, encourage it, frame it, and display it." (Sears, 2020).

Teaching Lifelong Values

Having a confident child that is willing to take risks and try new things, knowing that they have their parents' love no matter what is vital. But part of your job is also teaching your child to make good decisions, both for their own sake and for others. Here are some ways you can guide them into acquiring values.

Responsibility and Accountability

While sometimes these two terms are used as synonyms, when speaking about teaching a child responsibility it means letting them know in advance what is expected from them. Accountability, on the other hand, refers to accepting the consequences of one's actions or decisions, both the positive as well as the negative.

You give children responsibilities when you assign them duties they are capable of fulfilling. In that sense, you always have to consider the age of the child: You can't expect a toddler to make lunch, but you can ask them to set the table and thus, create in them a responsibility. If you are uncertain whether your toddler is too young to take any responsibilities at all, consider the Montessori philosophy, which suggests a list of age-appropriate activities (of course, if you have a child who has some motor development delays, you may want to offer them extra assistance or wait a little longer):

For two or three-year-olds, Montessori philosophy suggests (Zerfas, 2022)

- help to set the table
- put their dirty clothes in the hamper
- dust off whatever surface they can reach safely, such as the coffee table
- wipe up their spills
- wash their tricycle or scooter
- pick up their toys and put them away

- feed the family's pet
- water the plants
- help to prepare meals: Pour out the salad dressing, make a sandwich, help mix cookie dough or use their cutter, and so on

What's important is that you let the child try to do these things their way, it doesn't matter if they are not perfect: You are not looking for less work—actually, when a toddler "helps" it usually means *more* work for you!—you are looking forward to teaching them to become responsible. Again, think about it as an investment in the long run.

But giving them chores to do is only part of becoming a responsible person. While most parents are ready to ask their kids to help around the house, do their homework, or put away their toys, they fail at teaching them what happens if they refuse or give excuses (Lehman, n.d.):

Many parents either don't hold their kids accountable or don't follow through on the consequences once they set them, which in turn just promotes more irresponsibility. Once again, the child learns that his excuses and lies and justifications work for him in his effort to avoid responsibility for himself or his behavior.

This is where accountability comes in. If being responsible is being given a task, being accountable means accepting the consequences of not accomplishing that same task. In this sense, a positive parent will not jump to solve their child's problem or offer excuses. Instead, you want to provide them with tools for understanding what they did wrong, and trying to solve it, or else accepting the consequences of their wrongdoings.

When setting boundaries, positive parenting focuses on the Three F's: Firm, Fair, and Friendly (Iyanuoluwa, 2022). Being firm means that you set the rules in a clear tone, leaving no room for negotiation: "It's time to put away your toys and take a bath." Being friendly means that you still do it with love and respect, you don't yell, you don't punish your child, you simply let them know what's going to happen if they don't listen: "If you put away your toys now, we'll have more time to play in the bathtub and make some bubbles. If you take too long, you'll miss out." Being fair means that the consequences should be related to the mistake. In this example, if the child refuses to cooperate and they don't put their toys away, there will be no bubbles in their bath. You just give them a quick shower and take them out so they can put their toys away before bedtime. If they continue not to cooperate, you can let them know they'll also miss storytime.

But by no means you should punish them by taking all of their toys away from them! And neither should you give in, simply sigh, and put the toys away yourself with no consequence whatsoever. The consequences should be age-appropriate, anticipated, and what's most important, related to the kind of negative behavior or poor decision the child made. If you repeat this strategy, in time the toddler will know what's expected from them, and what happens if they don't do it. That's exactly what being accountable means.

Later in life, if your child didn't finish their science project and asks you to do it on their behalf the night before, teaching them accountability means you won't get them out of trouble by writing an excuse to their teachers. Instead, you can help them develop a strategy for apologizing, and how to negotiate an extension to their homework's deadline. Of course, they should also be ready to accept a bad grade if the teacher decides not to grant them such an extension!

Empathy

Empathy is the ability to put oneself in somebody else's situation, to understand how they must be feeling, and therefore, to act in consequence. Empathy connects people with one another, allowing us to feel what they are feeling. Empathy is the reason most humans can be kind, and help each other without waiting for something in return. Empathy makes us better people! And although the baby is born naturally selfish—at first, they can't even understand that they are separate individuals from their mothers—children can start developing empathy from a tender age, as long as their caregivers guide them appropriately.

By the time your toddler has turned 18 months, they start to develop a theory of mind: "This is when a toddler first realizes that, just as he has his own thoughts, feelings and goals, others have their own thoughts and ideas, and these may be different from his" (Parlakian, 2016). At this age, you can already teach them by example and simple actions on how to put themselves in someone else's shoes (Voran, 2021).

- **Be emphatic yourself.** Acknowledge your toddler's feelings. Once again, set the appropriate example! "I see you are crying because you can't find your doll. It's sad when toys get lost. Come on, I'll help you find it!"

- **Name their emotions.** Putting their feelings into words goes a long way toward a better understanding of every emotion, both theirs and others'. You can do it when watching a cartoon or reading a story: "See? Rubina is angry at her sister because she ate the red lollipop."

- **Address someone else's feelings.** If your toddler pushes another child in the sandbox, besides removing them from the situation, make them realize what they did was wrong not because they'll get into trouble, but because of what the other child feels: "Look at Jack's face. How does he look? Why do you think he's sad?" The idea is for them to realize they can cause others to feel things. You can—and should!—also use this mechanism for addressing positive feelings: "Did you see how Tim smiled when you lent him your rake? Why did he smile? It's nice to make other children happy!"

- **Link the other kid's feelings to theirs.** If your child caused another kid to cry, before making them apologize, you should address their own feelings. Once they understand that Jack is crying because he's sad, you can ask them if they ever felt the same. "What do you do when you are sad? What are the things that make you feel better?"

- **Help them make things right.** Teaching them to say 'sorry' is meaningless if they can't relate to what they did wrong in the first place.

Only after going through the previous step (relating to someone else's feelings), if possible, encourage your child to make amends. Maybe, instead of an awkward apology, he can give Jack a tissue for wiping his tears or share a cookie with him. When they grow a bit, you can explain to them that apologizing is a possible way of making the other person feel better and recognizing you did something wrong, but a forced apology by itself won't teach your toddler empathy .

Dealing With Frustration

Raising a confident, happy child means accepting they won't be happy *all the time*. This is one of the main differences between permissive parenting and positive parenting. You want your child to be happy, of course, but you understand that happiness doesn't equal automatic satisfaction. In fact, preventing your child from dealing with difficult situations will make things more challenging for them in the future. Life *is* difficult sometimes! They will bump into obstacles, resistance, and discomfort. You shouldn't overprotect your child because you won't always be there to get them out of trouble.

Let's start with a basic situation: Your toddler is cheerfully running in the park, and suddenly they trip and fall on their knees. Your first impulse is to rush and pick them up before they cry. Wait! Allow them to get up by themselves first. If they are hurt, they will cry and call for help. Assist them then, of course, and provide reassurance: "I saw you fell. Your knees probably hurt, it's okay to cry. But they will get better, and I'm sure you have a great time when you run." Sometimes, before you get to pick them up, they stand up again and keep running. If you rush to help them, you will be showing them you don't believe they were able to solve the problem by themselves.

The same applies to other situations in which they feel frustrated: Your toddler is upset because they can't put more than three blocks in a pile, and it goes down. Instead of showing them how to build a steady tower, help them to find a solution by themselves: "Oh, it looks tricky. Which block is bigger? What happens when you place it on top of the other one? I see…"

Addressing a toddler's feelings means acknowledging them, letting them know you see them, you notice them, and you care. But it doesn't mean you should make those unpleasant feelings disappear. In the same way, you should never scold or punish a toddler simply for being whiny or choleric. You should let them know that certain behaviors are inadmissible, but their feelings are always okay. In any case, you can offer them safe ways to express these feelings: Draw a picture of what makes them sad, or hit a pillow if they are feeling angry. It can also help you teach them relaxation techniques, such as taking a deep breath or picturing a green balloon inside their belly they can blow whenever they need to calm down.

Last but not least, remember it takes a long time for a toddler to learn to cope with frustration and other unpleasant feelings. Some adults still find it difficult! So always keep your expectations realistic, and don't forget to praise any improvement you notice, no matter how little it seems: "You stopped crying and now you are playing with your blocks again, I'm proud of you!" Your loving words will slowly turn into their inner voice: As they grow up, they'll learn to cope with frustration and become perseverant, something essential if you want to succeed in anything in life!

Chapter Takeaways

- The way you help your child build confidence has a direct impact not only on their current behavior but in all their future life. A child that has strong self-esteem develops into a healthy, confident teen who trusts their parents and their inner abilities.

- You can help your child become confident from an early age: Expressing unconditional love and acceptance, providing valuable encouragement (not empty praise), setting the example by displaying your self-confidence, and encouraging them to spend time doing something they are good at.

- Children make good decisions when they have learned to be responsible and accountable. Giving your toddler age-appropriate tasks is important, but even more, is making sure there are consequences if they don't fulfill their responsibilities.

- When setting up boundaries, remember the Three F's: Firm, Fair, and Friendly!

- Teaching your toddler empathy goes way beyond uttering a forced apology. You have to name their emotions and relate them to other people's.

- If you want your child to develop confidence, you can't go after them solving each and every difficulty they bump into. Accept that your toddler may not feel great all the time, teach them strategies for dealing with difficult emotions, and help them find a solution to their problems.

In our last chapter, we will see more ways in which you can create a deeper bond with your toddler, what activities you can share to further strengthen your connection, and how sustaining your positive relationship in time has all kinds of benefits for the parents as well.

Chapter 6

Parenting's a Journey—Enjoy the Ride!

And what has been hidden from the wise and the prudent been revealed in the mouth of the toddlers.
–Bob Marley

At first, when my first child was born, I felt so overwhelmed with my new responsibilities that I forgot to enjoy being a mum. Even after embracing the positive parenting philosophy, I believed that it was all about teaching the child. But once you take your focus out of misbehaving issues, when your positive parenting strategies start showing off some results, I suggest you pay attention to how much your toddler can actually teach *you*!

That's right: Sustaining a positive relationship with your toddler in time will make *your* whole life richer, healthier, and happier. You should not raise a child at the expense of your own well-being! Being a parent is tiresome, you don't need to tell me, but it is also a wonderful adventure worth living.

What kind of impact does positive parenting have on a marriage? How does spending more time together benefit the parents as well as the children? Is it possible to protect the secure atmosphere of your home once you get used to positive parenting? How can we continue improving our relationship with our toddlers as time goes by? In this chapter, we'll find the answers to these questions and more.

The Importance of Your Partner

Back then, when I first started reading about positive parenting, the first thing I did was share some of the most significant discoveries with my husband, Greg. Luckily, I must say he almost immediately got on board! Before this happened, when we first became parents, we had our disagreements. Greg reacted way less than I did, he's by nature calmer. He grew up with authoritarian parents, and he subconsciously refused to become one himself. When Lanie was a young toddler, he was always giving in and excusing all the bad behavior with the typical "She'll grow up someday!" This left me feeling lonely when it came to setting boundaries and ground rules. I overreacted often and I turned into this grumpy mum I didn't want to become.

After learning about positive parenting, both Greg and I started noticing which were the things we needed to change. Fortunately, we could learn from one another: He taught me the value of kindness and being caring even when I didn't feel like it; I taught him that Lanie needed clear limits because if we didn't teach them, she would learn them the hard way! To sum up, while we were reflecting on what kind of parents we wanted to be, we both discovered we had a huge common goal: Both for my husband and me, our family was the Number One Priority!

The truth is, you have to be on the same page when it comes to parenting. You may not agree on everything, but you have to communicate and find a middle ground: "One of the positive parenting solutions is to discuss what you each have strong feelings about and see where you can compromise on certain parenting decisions" (Jacobson, 2020).

It's important that you set the rules and the consequences together, and that you back each other up. This is especially necessary when the parents are separated, divorced, or spending most of their time apart (perhaps because of their work schedules). Children can tell when their parents disagree on something, and they will take advantage of it. The same happens when parents argue in front of their children. If you need to discuss something with your partner, do it in private. In front of your kids, always show that you have joined forces!

If your marriage breaks apart, you can remain positive parents. You both must keep on the same page, and none of you should speak ill of the other in front of the children. Any difference or conflict between the adults should remain private, and you both shall do your best to keep providing the child with both parents' unconditional love and a meaningful connection. Of course, "the exception to this is if you feel that your partner is harming your kids either physically or emotionally" (Jacobson, 2020). In that case, you will do what it takes to protect your children.

If you are a single parent, on one hand, you don't need to agree with anyone when making the rules. On the other hand, it is always important to have someone you trust that can support you emotionally so you can be there for your child—they can be your parents, a sibling, a close friend, or a new partner.

Benefits of Positive Parenting for the Relationship

As we have seen, "left unchecked, parenting differences can cause marital problems which can, in turn, disrupt the entire family" (Jacobson, 2020). The good news is, once you start implementing the principles of positive parenting, the benefits will not only reach the child but their parents and their relationship as well! If you are consistent about teaching your child with the example, your marriage or relationship can improve in the following aspects.

Communication

Being more open to talking about your feelings with your child can also help you better communicate with your spouse. Talking frankly about each other's parenting expectations can lead to more open talk. Communication is the key to compromise and finding common ground both for parenting as well as for other aspects of your relationship as well!

Connection

Do you remember how we stated that it only takes 10 minutes a day to actively engage with your toddler? Or the importance of the five to one ratio when it comes to positive interactions? If you start applying the same principles to your marriage, you'll find that the relationship heals, you get emotionally attached, and you enjoy your time together! You don't even need to spend money on a babysitter. Put the children to bed, turn off the cell phones and the television, and just talk.

Empathy

If you can practice empathy with your toddler to understand the storm of unnamed emotions they are still too little to process by themselves, you can also try to empathize with your spouse. The main difference is that, because you both are adults, you can vividly describe your emotions so the other one can understand them. And because you want to explain how you are feeling to your partner, this helps you put into words your feelings, so you can handle them better.

Some time ago, if I had a bad day at work I used to come home too sensitive, and any setback could make me upset or emotional. Now, I'm used to talking to my husband about whatever happened that day, and this prevents me from taking it out on him or the kids. At the same time, because I tell them how I feel, both Greg and the children know when I need some space, and leave me alone if I just need to unwind for a while.

Flexibility

Positive parenting has also made us more flexible, not only as parents but as people, too. We argue less, and when we do, we are careful with each other. We have learned to accept our children the way they are while giving them guide rules at the same time so they can turn into the best possible version of themselves. And maybe without even realizing it, we also transformed—and grew.

Sustaining a Positive Relationship With Your Toddler

We have already explained how positive parenting benefits children in the long run, by making them more confident, secure, independent, better at making decisions, and more open to communicating their emotions. Later in life, they do better in school, they are more optimistic, and in their teenage years they have overall better mental health and succumb less to peer pressure, so they are less likely to fall into damaging behaviors.

So positive parenting turns out to be a better quality of life for your kids. But what if I told you that sustaining a positive relationship with them is also great for you? Let's further explore other ways in which you can sustain a positive relationship with your toddler and all the benefits that some of these practices can offer to parents.

Spending More Time Together

I insist: Quality time is more important than quantity. However, once you become a positive parent, you'll find yourself spending *more* time with your toddler, whether interacting with them on one-on-one time (which, by the way, is a boost for your confidence in your parenting skills, as you see your child being happy and reaching for you with a big smile), communicating with them, or simply keeping an eye on them while they explore their surroundings during their time playing outside.

People with older children who practice positive parenting are motivated into going to their child's ballet recital, their soccer practice, or organizing lots of fun activities for them and their friends. Because you have a genuine interest in understanding your child and you respect them as a person, you will start considering those moments of active parenting an investment in their future, and not an obligation you need to fulfill. And let me tell you, I was that mum who was always scrolling through social media because of fear of missing out (FOMO). Once I focused on looking at my children and creating happy, unique moments with them, those long minutes doing nothing but looking at other people's posts and endless notifications started to feel like a waste of time!

Because I want my children to stay away from screens and enjoy the outdoors, I do the same, and it has made wonders for my anxiety. And we all sleep better at night after spending some time playing outside and breathing fresh air. And ever since the temper tantrums and the behavior problems became less frequent, we also dedicate several weekends to taking trips or going places with the children. Now I no longer fear how they will react! Sure, they still misbehave now and then, but I have gotten rid of the anxiety it generated for me now that I'm more confident in my parenting skills.

I still value my career, and working outside my house means I don't get to spend all day with my children. You don't need to do so either. But I must admit that some time ago, I dreaded the constant tantrums at home so much that, in contrast, the hours I spent at work seemed like an escape. So I would often linger doing unimportant little tasks to arrive home a little later. I wouldn't admit it at that time; since I was so ashamed by the feeling I was not good enough as a mother. But I often told myself I needed just a little more time to take photocopies or to finish correcting papers since at home I didn't have peace and silence.

I don't do that anymore: Now that I enjoy being with my children, I leave work on time to get home early and stay longer with them. That also generated an unexpected but most welcomed consequence: I'm more productive than ever during my working hours. Because I want to get home early, I no longer procrastinate and leave stuff for the last minute.

Protecting Your Peaceful Environment

There are some strategies you can implement at home to surround yourself and your family with a peaceful environment. If your home has a calm atmosphere, it will help you and your toddler keep your inner peace as well. Here are some suggestions:

- **Make sure everyone is onboard.** If you don't get to spend every hour with your toddler, and you need to leave them some hours with a babysitter or a family member, check that they are aware of your parenting approach. Your toddler could get frustrated and annoyed if somebody starts giving them time-outs or taking away their dessert all of a sudden! You don't need to give your mother-in-law a whole lecture on why positive parenting is the best approach and its many advantages, only let them know the way in which you handle tantrums and misbehaving and ask her to respect your choice.

- **Create a screen-free place, especially for relaxing.** Make sure there is a special place in your house that has little stimulus and offers the perfect conditions for relaxing. It doesn't have to be a whole room, it can be a corner with cushions and a lamp with a soft light. "If we build in a physical space for our stress-soothing habits, we have a physical reminder, as well as a facilitator, to help us maintain the motivation to keep these habits in our lives" (Scott, 2021). Something to take into account: Keep it technology-free! You can take your toddler to that place whenever they are overexcited, but you too can benefit from five minutes of quiet time.

- **Say yes to charts!** Placing attractive, colorful charts in visible places in the house may help your toddler remember routines and habits. A special chart for their morning routine, another one for their bedtime routine, and such. Make sure you include them when you create those charts: For example, they can color the drawings with their crayons. By the way, some parents also appreciate visual help: For example, keeping a list of positive statements on your night table can remind you to say them often to your toddler.

- **Create your special habits.** Together with your partner, you can come up with unique family routines to strengthen the bond with your children. It can be anything you all enjoy, from wearing pajamas for lunch on Saturdays to dancing in a circle whenever a specific song is played. You can invent chants, rhymes, or games for playing during the car ride. The goal is to create a special family code that makes you feel united!

Guilt-Free and Blame-Free Family Lifetime!

One of the main advantages of positive parenting is that it teaches children to become responsible and accountable for their actions and choices. In previous chapters, we have already mentioned some strategies, such as avoiding punishment and opting for natural consequences. Along the same line, you should never blame your toddler if they break the rules. Tina Louise Ballodi, a mum of two girls, refers to this practice as "sounding like an owl" (Ballodi, 2015):

WHOOO? WHOOO? WHOOO? WHOOO? How many times a day do parents and families walk around the house sounding like an owl saying, Who did this? (...) I can hear myself, almost as if I am floating above myself watching and listening. It is such a habit to say, Who did this? There are times that I have to catch myself in the act as I am saying it.

What can you do instead of blaming? You simply mention that the rules have been broken and somebody has to become accountable. For example

- Instead of "How come you didn't make your bed?" try: "I noticed your bed is still undone."

- Instead of "Who let the lights of the toilet on?" try: "I see the lights are on and there's nobody in the toilet..."

- Instead of "You were supposed to feed the cat!" try: "The cat looks hungry, and her bowl is empty."

This way, you are addressing not even the poor behavior but the visible consequences of it. Instead of making the child feel guilty and ashamed, just by selecting your words carefully, you are providing them an opportunity to make amends and to become accountable for their actions.

Something important is that you should stop blaming *yourself*. As far as I can remember, being a mum has provided me with huge amounts of guilt: No matter what I did, it was never good enough. Positive parenting focuses on your achievements as well as your children's. It becomes natural as you get used to it. Think of it as a mindfulness exercise. You won't accomplish it every day, and you shouldn't blame yourself if, for example, you ever get distracted during those minutes you decided to connect with your toddler one on one. At least you are trying! Pat yourself on the back if you managed to simply look at your toddler playing without picking up your phone, even if you didn't feel you were 100% there that time.

Finally, don't give anyone outside your home the power to make you feel guilty about your parenting decisions. Your house, your rules! And no, I'm not going to tell you to become an authoritarian person. But this principle should apply to any external visitor that criticizes the way in which you talk to your toddler on how you handle conflict or misbehaving when you are at home. If your parents or your friends come to visit, and they start saying things like "Back then, children would listen when adults talked," or "If I were you, I'd punish them for doing so and so…" Well, you can apply the Three F's and be friendly, firmly, and fairly, remind them that this is *your* family and these are the rules that you follow at home. Don't let friends or family, much less total strangers, mom-shame you in any way!

Chapter Takeaways

- Positive parenting has advantages not only

for your toddler's development but for your well-being as well!

- It's essential to be on the same page with your partner when raising your child. This is even more vital if you two are no longer a loving couple.

- Positive parenting can help you become more communicative, get in touch with your emotions, be more empathic, and be more flexible also in your adult life.

- When you start enjoying being around your toddler, you'll find out you spend more time with them without even realizing it. At least, the time spent together with your child will not feel like an obligation but like an investment.

- To protect the atmosphere you have achieved at home, there are many things you can do, such as making sure you inform other caregivers of your parenting approach, using charts for routines, offering your toddler (and yourself) a calm, quiet space, and creating special family habits.

- Being a positive parent means getting rid of unpleasant feelings such as blame, shame, and guilt, both for your children as well as yourself.

As we have seen, sustaining a great relationship with your toddler will not only have positive consequences on their lives, development, and happiness but also on yours! Becoming a parent is the most important decision you have taken in life: Enjoying parenting will make your life enjoyable as well!

Conclusion

Children are not adults-in-the-making; they are not clay to be molded. They are children, and that is that. Our task is to wonder at them, to learn about ourselves through our relationships with them. –Robin Grille

Here we are, at the end of the path! I wrote this book to share my experience with all of you who are struggling to raise your toddler and can't wait for this hard stage to end. It's a time of constant defiance, as your child is no longer a baby and wants to prove themselves an independent little person, but still lacks enough tools and maturity to recognize and express the emotions that overwhelm them. It doesn't help when so many people refer to this stage as "toddler terror" or "the terrible two's." I won't deny it's challenging and can be hard sometimes, but you too can learn to enjoy spending time with your toddler and embracing these years of their life with the aid of positive parenting.

My oldest daughter is no longer a toddler. Lanie is six now, and she has become an independent, cheerful, optimistic, talkative, and caring schoolgirl. I look back to those days in which I struggled so hard not to lose it, and sometimes I get sad because I feel somehow I missed out. Currently, I'm very open to communicating with Lanie, and when I tell her how sorry I am for that time I lost my temper right before her birthday party, she wisely states: "Mommy, you did the best you could!"

Louis and Jack, my twins, are three years old and are rapidly growing from being toddlers to becoming preschoolers. They both can talk already, they are energetic, they no longer take naps every day (despite every table chart stating they *should* be napping...), and their temper tantrums are rare nowadays. Still, they are a handful because they are both curious and have a tendency to break the rules, so both my husband and I put a lot of effort into correcting them by making them understand the natural consequences of their actions... And they constantly remind us that being a parent is a 24/7 job!

And still, ever since we turned to positive parenting, we find out things got smoother. We no longer nag all day. We practice being empathic and try to relate our children's behavior to their age to keep realistic expectations. At the same time, we set clear rules and explain to them why they should respect them. Our children are better adjusted to their morning and bedtime routines, and we have found a way to keep calm most of the time. We all spend less time in front of the TV and more hours playing outside. We have started to grow our vegetables in the backyard, and the household chores have become easier now that we have three little pairs of helpful hands we can count on.

And if positive parenting worked for me it's not out of chance: Science backs it up as one of the best parenting styles anyone can adopt. Now that you have read so many strategies, remember you can summarize them in some simple principles. If you follow these, then all of the tips and strategies will flow:

- Every child is naturally good: A child's mischief is either a call for attention, an accumulation of emotions they are yet to learn to express, or ignorance of the expected behavior.

- Every child is looking for connection and meaningfulness.

- Children should be treated with respect: Teach them, don't tame them.
- When disciplining your child, praise and encourage positive behavior instead of punishing bad behavior.
- Guide them to understand the natural consequences of their decisions, both of the negative ones as well as the positive ones.
- Apply the Three F's: Be firm, fair, and friendly.
- Always give your child unconditional love.

It's never too late to start implementing positive parenting. You should start making the first steps today. Perhaps you already are! Take a deep breath, be patient, and understand it will take some time. Creating new habits takes effort, consistency, and perseverance. The results won't show in a day or two.

Think of yourself as being a "toddler" as well: When deciding to change your approach towards parenting, you too are taking little steps, you too stumble across the obstacles, and you too are exploring a whole new world that can sometimes be scary. Besides, you should accept you won't be able to be a positive parent 100% of the time. Sometimes you'll still lose it. Sometimes you'll go back to your usual ways, scold your child, and feel sorry afterward. We all still need to unlearn some of our old habits that don't work. But when we give them the chance and we listen to them, children can become our best teachers.

Spend as much quality time as possible together. Let your child teach you how to become the best possible version of yourself. Now they are toddlers, but soon they will become scholars who need to be responsible for studying for their English tests, or teenagers dealing with peer pressure. You want them to trust you, and to come to you whenever they need advice, help, or simply a warm, long hug.

As a positive parent, become a leader and guide them into becoming confident, curious, independent, caring, and responsible human beings who are capable of making the right choices knowing that they'll have your unconditional love.

And enjoy the ride!

About The Author

Alma Aldrich is a 32-year-old mom who lives in Maryland. She has been married for the past eight years. She and her husband Greg are proud parents of Elaine (aged six), and twin boys Louis and Jack (aged three). When she is not working as a music teacher or taking care of her kids, she enjoys working out, taking care of her garden, and practicing mindfulness.

References

Altrogge, S. (2019, April 30). *12 morning and evening routines that will set up each day for success.* Zapier.

American Psychological Association (2019, December 12). *Digital guidelines: Promoting healthy technology use for children.* APA.Org.

Ballodi, T. (2015, June 6). . Kids in The House. https://www.kidsinthehouse.com/blogs/tina-louise-balodi/how-to-stop-sounding-like-an-owl-create-a-blame-free-home

Christiano, D. (2019, September 27). *Which parenting type is right for you?* Healthline.

Davies, A. (2020, March 9). *Disciplining toddlers: Why time-ins are the new time-outs.* The Bump. https://www.thebump.com/a/toddler-time-ins

Dewar, G. (2017). *The authoritative parenting style: An evidence-based guide*. Parenting Science.

Eanes, R. (2016). *Positive parenting: An essential guide*. TarcherPerigee.

Geddes, J (2022, June 21). *How to use the bedtime fading sleep training method*. What to Expect.

Grille, R. (2018) *Parenting for a peaceful world*. Kindle Edition.

Grose, M. (2017, February 13). *Confidence-building strategies every parent should know*. Parenting Ideas. https://www.parentingideas.com.au/blog/confidence-building-strategies-every-parent-should-know/

Hart, L. (1995). *The winning family: Increasing self-esteem in your children and yourself*. Celestial Arts.

Holmes, K (2016). *Why every parent should know the magic 5:1 ratio – And how to do it*. Happy You, Happy Family.

Houston, W. (1985) "Greatest Love of All" [song]. On *Whitney Houston*. Arista.

Iyanuoluwa, F. (2022, January 14). *The 3 Fs of effective parenting*. Schools Compass. https://schoolscompass.com.ng/blog/2022/01/14/the-3-fs-of-effective-parenting/

Jacobson, T. (2020, March 17). *Top 5 positive parenting solutions – Finding common ground with your spouse*. Marriage.com. https://www.marriage.com/advice/parenting/positive-parenting-solutions/

Kennedy, L. (2020, November 6). *11 positive parenting strategies you need to start using*. Prodigy.

Lehman, J. (n.d.) *Teach your child responsibility – 7 tips to get started*. Empowering Parents. https://www.empoweringparents.com/article/teach-your-child-responsibility-7-tips-to-get-started/

Leo, P. (2007). *Connection parenting: Parenting through connection instead of coercion, through love instead of fear*. Wyatt-MacKenzie Publishing; 2nd edition

Li, P. (2022, June 28). *Positive parenting – The definitive guide and 9 essential tips*. Parenting for Brain. https://www.parentingforbrain.com/what-is-positive-parenting/

Li, P. (2022, August 20). *Reactive parenting – What it is & how to overcome*. Parenting for Brain.

Lively, S. (2014, July 16). *30 joyful ways to connect with your child in 10 minutes*. One Time Through. https://onetimethrough.com/joyful-ways-to-connect/

Mapp, S., Gabel, S.G. (2019) It is easier to build strong children than to repair broken men. J. Hum. Rights Soc. Work 4, 145–146.

Marley, B. (1979) "Forever Loving Jah" [song]. On *Uprising* [album]. Tuff Gong/Island

Mayo Clinic. (2018). *Postpartum depression*. Mayo Clinic.

McCready, A. (2015). *Picky eaters. How to change habits WITHOUT causing a food fight*. Positive Parenting Solutions.

McCready, A. (2021, December 9). *Here's what makes 'positive parenting' different—And why experts say it's one of the best parenting styles*. CNBC.

Morin, A. (2022, September 2). *How to use positive reinforcement to improve behavior*. VeryWell Family. https://www.verywellfamily.com/positive-reinforcement-child-behavior-1094889

Morrison, T. (2016). *God help the child*. Vintage.

Mueller, S. (2012). *Are you a reactive parent or a proactive parent?* Educating Today. http://www.educatingtoday.com/are-you-a-reactive-parent-or-a-proactive-parent/

Mulroy, Z. (2016, July 26). *The parenting trick recommended by experts—Even though Prince William got told off for it.* Mirror.co.uk.

Nelsen, J. (2006). *Positive discipline: The classic guide to helping children develop self-discipline, responsibility, cooperation, and problem-solving skills.* Ballantine Books.

Parlakian, R. (2016, February 1). *How to help your child develop empathy.* Zero to Three. https://www.zerotothree.org/resource/how-to-help-your-child-develop-empathy/

Phillips, R. (2014, November 9). *Toddlers 101: Understanding toddler development.* Parents.

The Pragmatic Parent (2016). *Why you should stop saying good job and what to say instead.* The Pragmatic Parent. https://www.thepragmaticparent.com/stopsayinggoodjob/

Punkoney, S. (2012). *Fine motor practice with scooping and pouring.* Stay at Home Educator. https://stayathomeeducator.com/fine-motor-practice-with-scooping-and-pouring/

Raising Children Network (2019). *Outdoor play.* Raising Children Network. https://raisingchildren.net.au/toddlers/play-learning/outdoor-play/outdoor-play

Richfield, S. (2019, August 2). *Impact of a reactive parent on a child's self-control.* HealthyPlace.

Rowell, R. (2014, June). *The disappearing chair—Sleep training method.* My Baby Sleep Guide. http://www.mybabysleepguide.com/2014/06/the-disappearing-chair-sleep-training.html

Russell, L. (2021, December 9). *Reactive parenting: 5 simple actions to break the cycle.* They Are The Future.

Scher, H. (2022, June 22). *7 common toddler behaviors and what they mean.* Parents.

Scott, E. (2021, July 16). *How to make your home more peaceful.* VeryWell Mind. https://www.verywellmind.com/elements-of-a-peaceful-home-3144735

Sears, W. (2020). *12 ways to raise a confident child.* Ask Dr. Sears. https://www.askdrsears.com/topics/parenting/child-rearing-and-development/12-ways-help-your-child-build-self-confidence/

Smokowski, P., Bacallao, M., Cotter, K., & Evans, C. (2014, June). "The effects of positive and negative parenting practices on adolescent mental health outcomes in a multicultural sample of rural youth". 46(3) DOI:. Source:

University of California (2018). *In memoriam. Diana B Baumrind. Research psychologist, emerita.* Academic Senate.

Voran, J. (2021). *Forcing toddlers to apologize doesn't teach empathy—Here's what does.* The Everymom. https://theeverymom.com/how-to-teach-empathy-to-toddlers/

Wilde, O. (2007). *Epigrams of Oscar Wilde.* Wordsworth Editions.

Zeltser, F. (2021, June 29). *A psychologist shares the 4 styles of parenting—and the type that researchers say is the most successful.* CNBC. Make It.

Zerfas, K. (2022, March 11). *Children as contributing members of the mome.* Greenspring Montessori School. https://greenspringmontessori.org/montessori-chores/

Printed in Great Britain
by Amazon